PREFACE TO AMERICAN EDITION

THE NOBILITY OF THE SEX PROBLEM

Of all the problems which the alert and curious mind of modern man is considering, none occupies him more than that of the relations of the sexes. This is natural. It touches us all and we have made rather a mess of it! We want to know why, and we want to do better. We resent being the sport of circumstance and perhaps we are beginning to understand that this instinct of sex which has been so great a cause of suffering and shame and has been treated as a subject fit only for furtive whispers or silly jokes, is in fact one of the greatest powers in human nature, and that its misuse is indeed "the expense of spirit in a waste of shame."

It is not the abnormal or the bizarre that interests most of us to-day. It is not into the by-ways of vice that we seek to penetrate. It is the normal exercise of a normal instinct by normal people that interests us: and it is of this that I have tried to write and speak. The curiosities of depravity are for the physician and the psychologist to discuss and cure. Ordinary men and women want first to know how to live ordinary human lives on a higher level and after a nobler pattern than before. They want, I think,—and I want,—to grow up, but to grow rightly, beautifully, humanely.

And I believe the first essential is to realize that the sex-problem, as it is called, is the problem of something noble, not something base. It is not a "disagreeable duty" to know our own natures and understand our own instincts: it is a joy. The sex-instinct is not "the Fall of Man"; neither is it an instance of divine wisdom on which moralists could, if they had only been consulted in time, greatly have improved. It is a thing noble in essence. It is the development of the higher, not the lower, creation. It is the asexual which is the lower, and the sexually differentiated which is the higher organism.

In the humbler ranks of being there is no sex, and in a sense no death. The organism is immortal because—strange paradox—it is not yet alive enough to die. But as we pass from the lower to the higher, we pass from the less individual to the more individual; from asexual to sexual. And with this change comes that great rhythm by which life and death succeed each other, and death is the *cost* of life, and to bring life into the world means sacrifice; and—as we rise higher still—to sustain life means prolonged and altruistic love. This is the history of sex and of procreation, a history associated with the rising of humanity in the scale of being, a history not so much of his physical as of his spiritual growth.

By what an irony have we come to associate the instinct of sex with all that is bestial and shameful!

It has happened because the corruption of the best is the worst. I always want to remind people of this truism when they have *first* come into contact with sex in some horrible and shameful way. That is one of the greatest misfortunes that can happen to any of us, and unfortunately it happens to many. Boys and girls are allowed to grow up in ignorance. The girls perhaps know nothing till they have to know all. The boys learn from grimy sources. I was speaking on this subject at one of our great universities the other day, and afterwards many of the men came and talked to me privately.

With hardly a single exception they said to me—"Our parents told us nothing. We have never heard sex spoken of except in a dirty way."

It is difficult for us, in such a case, to realize that sex is not a dirty thing. It *can* only be realized, I think, by remembering that the corruption of the best is the worst, and that we can measure by the hideousness of debased and depraved sexuality, the greatness and the wonder of sex love.

This is to me the great teaching of Christ about sex. Other great religious teachers—some of them very great indeed—have thought and taught contemptuously of our animal nature. "He spake of the temple of His body." That is sublime! That is the whole secret. And that is why vice is horrible: because it is the desecration, not of a hovel or a shop, of a marketplace or a place of business: but of a temple.

Christ, I am told, told us nothing about sex. He did not need to tell us anything but "Your body is the Temple of the Holy Spirit."

It is my belief that in appealing to an American public I shall be appealing to those who are ready to face the subject of the relations of the sexes with perfect frankness and with courage. America is still a country of experiments—a country adventurous enough to make experiments, and to risk making mistakes. That is the only spirit in which it is possible to make anything at all; and though the mistakes we may make in a matter which so deeply and tragically affects human life must be serious, and we must with corresponding seriousness weigh every word we say, and take the trouble to think harder and more honestly than we have perhaps ever thought before; yet I believe that we must above all have courage. Human nature is sound and men and women do, on the whole, want to do what is right. The great impulse of sex is part of our very being, and it is not base. Passion is essentially noble and those who are incapable of it are the weaker, not the stronger. If then we have light to direct our course, we shall learn to direct it wisely, for indeed this is our desire.

Such is my creed. My prayer is for "more light." And my desire to take my part in spreading it.

A. MAUDE ROYDEN.

April, 1922.

CONTENTS

I.—THE OLD PROBLEM INTENSIFIED BY THE DISPROPORTION OF THE SEXES

II.—A SOLUTION OF THE PROBLEM OF THE UNMARRIED

III.—CONSIDERATION OF OTHER SOLUTIONS OF THE PROBLEM OF THE DISPROPORTION OF THE SEXES

IV.—THE TRUE BASIS OF MORALITY

V.—THE MORAL STANDARD OF THE FUTURE: WHAT SHOULD IT BE?

VI.—A PLEA FOR LIGHT

VII.—FRIENDSHIP

VIII.—MISUNDERSTANDINGS

IX.—FURTHER MISUNDERSTANDINGS: THE NEED FOR SEX CHIVALRY

X.—"THE SIN OF THE BRIDEGROOM"

XI.—COMMON-SENSE AND DIVORCE LAW REFORM

I

THE OLD PROBLEM INTENSIFIED BY THE DISPROPORTION OF THE SEXES

"There has arisen in society, a figure which is certainly the most mournful, and in some respects the most awful, upon which the eye of the moralist can dwell. That unhappy being whose very name is a shame to speak; who counterfeits with a cold heart the transports of affection, and submits herself as the passive instrument of lust; who is scorned and insulted as the vilest of her sex, and doomed for the most part to disease and abject wretchedness and an early death, appears in every eye as the perpetual symbol of the degradation and sinfulness of man. Herself the supreme type of vice, she is ultimately the most efficient guardian of virtue. But for her the unchallenged purity of countless happy homes would be polluted, and not a few who, in the pride of their untempted chastity, think of her with an indignant shudder, would have known the agony of remorse and despair. She remains while creeds and civilisations rise and fall, the eternal priestess of humanity, blasted for the sins of the people."

Lecky's *History of European Morals*, Chap. V.

One of the many problems which have been intensified by the war is the problem of the relations of the sexes. Difficult as it has always been, the difficulty inevitably becomes greater when there is a grave disproportion—an excess in numbers of one sex over the other. And in this country, whereas there was a disproportion of something like a million more women than men before the war broke out, there is now a disproportion of about one and three-quarter millions.

This accidental and (I believe) temporary difficulty—a difficulty not "natural" and necessary to human life, but artificial and peculiar to certain conditions which may be altered—does not, of course, create the problem we have to deal with: but it forces that problem on our attention by sheer force of suffering inflicted on so large a scale. It compels us to ask ourselves on what we base, and at what we value the moral standard which, if it is to be preserved, must mean a tremendous sacrifice on the part of so large a number of women as is involved in their acceptance of life-long celibacy.

There is no subject on which it is more difficult to find a common ground than this. To some people it seems to be immoral even to ask the question—on what are your moral standards based? To others what we call our "moral standards" are so obviously absurd and "unnatural" that the question has for them no meaning. And between these extremes there are so many varieties of opinion that one can take nothing as generally accepted by men and women.

I want, therefore, to leave aside the ordinary conventions—not because they are necessarily bad, but because they are not to my purpose, which is to discover whether there is a real morality which we can justify to ourselves without appeal to any authority however great, or to any tradition however highly esteemed: a morality which is based on the real needs, the real aspirations of humanity itself.

And I begin by calling your attention to the morality of Jesus of Nazareth, not because He is divine, but because He was a great master of the human heart, and more than others "knew what was in man."

You will notice at once the height of His morality—the depth of His mercy. He demands such purity of spirit, such loyalty of heart, that the most loyal of His disciples shrank appalled: "Whosoever shall look upon a woman to lust after her hath committed adultery with her already in his heart." ... "Whosoever shall put away his wife and marry another, committeth adultery against her." From such a standard Christ's disciples shrank—"If the case of the man be so with his wife, it is not good to marry." And one evangelist almost certainly inserted in this absolute prohibition the exception—"Saving for the cause of fornication"—feeling that the Master *could* not have meant anything else. But, in fact, there is little doubt that Jesus did both say and mean that marriage demanded lifelong fidelity on either side; just as He really taught that a lustful thought was adultery in the sight of God.

But if Christendom has been staggered at the austerity of Christ's morality not less has it been shocked at the quality of His mercy. His gentleness to the sensual sinner has been compared, with amazement, to the sternness of His attitude to the sins of the spirit. Not the profligate or the harlot but the Pharisee and the scribe were those who provoked His sternest rebukes. And perhaps the most characteristic of all His dealings with such matters was that incident of the woman taken in adultery, when He at once reaffirmed the need of absolute chastity for men—demand undreamed of by the woman's accusers—and put aside the right to condemn which in all that assembly He alone could claim—"Neither do I condemn thee; go, and sin no more."

Having then in mind this most lofty and compassionate of moralists, let us turn to the problem of to-day. Here are nearly 2,000,000 women who, if the austere demands of faithful monogamy are to be obeyed, will never know the satisfaction of a certain physical need. Now it is the desire of every normal human being to satisfy all his instincts. And this is as true of women as of men. What I have to say applies indeed to many men to-day, for many men are unable to marry because they have been so broken by war —or otherwise—so shattered or maimed or impoverished that they do not feel justified in marrying. But I want to emphasize with all my power that the hardness of enforced celibacy presses as cruelly on women as on men. Women, difficult as some people find it to believe, are human beings; and because women are so, they want work, and interest, and love—both given and received—and children, and, in short, the satisfaction of every *human* need. The idea that existence is enough for them—that they need not work, and do not suffer if their sex instincts are repressed or starved—is a convenient but most cruel illusion. People often tell me, and nearly always unconsciously *assume,* that women have no sex hunger—no sex needs at all until they marry, and that even then their need is not at all so imperious as men's, or so hard to repress. Such people are nearly always either men, or women who have married young and happily and borne many children, and had a very full and interesting outside life as well! Such women will assure me with the utmost complacency that the sex-instincts of a woman are very easily controllable, and that it is preposterous to speak as if their repression really cost very much. I think with bitterness of that age-long repression, of its unmeasured cost; of the gibe contained in the phrase "old maid," with all its implication of a narrowed life, a prudish mind, an acrid tongue, an embittered disposition. I think of the imbecilities in which the repressed instinct has sought its pitiful baffled release, of the adulation lavished on a parrot, a cat, a lap-dog; or of the emotional "religion," the parson-worship, on which every fool is clever enough to sharpen his wit. And all these cramped and stultified lives have not availed to make the world understand that women have had to pay for their celibacy!

"The toad beneath the harrow knows
 Exactly where each tooth-point goes.
The butterfly beside the road
 Preaches contentment to that toad."

Modern psychology is lifting the veil to-day from the suffering which repression causes. It is a pity that its most brilliant exponents should ascribe to a single instinct—however potent—*all* the ills that afflict mankind, for such one-sidedness defeats its own object; but, at least, the modern psychologist is trying to show us "exactly where each tooth-point goes" in the repression of the sex-instinct among women as among men. Nor does the fact that the *tabu* of society has actually in many cases enabled a woman to inhibit the development of her own nature, obviate the fact that she does so at great cost, even when she least understands what she does.

I affirm this, and with insistence, that the normal—the average—woman sacrifices a great deal if she accepts life-long celibacy. She sacrifices quite as much as a man. In those cases—too frequent even now—where she is not educated or expected to earn her own living or to have a career, I maintain that she loses more than a man who is expected to work. I do not say, and I do not believe, that passion in a woman is the same as in a man, or that they suffer in precisely the same way. I believe indeed that if men and women understood each other a little better they would hurt each other a good deal less. But I am persuaded that we shall not even begin to reach a wise morality so long as we persist in basing our demands on the imbecile assumption that women suffer nothing or little by the unsatisfaction of the sex side of their nature.

I emphasize this point here, because it is involved in the present state of affairs. I have reminded you that there are nearly 2,000,000 women whose lives are to be considered. If the number were quite small, it might comfortably be assumed that the women who remained unmarried were those who, in any case, had no vocation for marriage. For it is, of course, true that there are such women, as there are such men. The normal man and woman desire marriage and parenthood, and are fitted for it; but there are always exceptions who either do not desire it, or, desiring it, feel bound to put it aside at the call of some other vocation, which they feel to be supremely theirs, and which is not compatible with marriage. They sacrifice; but they do so joyfully, not for repression, but for a different life, another vocation. And where the number of the unmarried is small, it may without essential injustice be supposed that these are the natural celibates.

But you cannot suppose that of 2,000,000! Among the number how many are young widows, girls engaged to marry men now dead, and how many whose *natural* vocation was marriage, motherhood, home-making, and all that is meant by such things as these? If this be the normal vocation of the normal woman how many of these have been deprived of all that seemed to them to make life worth living? Is it astonishing if they rebel? If they determine to snatch at anything that yet lies in their grasp? If they affirm "the right to motherhood" when they want children, or the satisfaction of the sex-instinct when that need becomes imperious?

If we are to say to such women—"The normal life is denied to you, not by your fault, or because you do not need it, but because we have unfortunately been obliged to sacrifice in war the men who should have been your mates: and we now invite you in the interests of morality to accept as your lot perpetual virginity"—it is not difficult to imagine their reply: "What is this morality in whose interests you ask so huge a sacrifice? Is it worth such a price? Is the whole community willing to pay it, or is it exacted from us alone? And on what, in the end, is it based?"

The answer to this question is often given to the young, even before the question arises; and it is given in the lives of men and women. The lives of those who are nobly celibate, or nobly married, are in themselves so moving a plea, that few who have been closely in contact with them are left untouched. It is the ideal realized that is the best defence of the ideal. But let us admit that, too often, the actual marriage is a very pitiful comment on our morality, and celibacy either a mere pretence or a very mean and pinched reality. What answer then shall we give to the rising generation which questions us—"On what do you base your moral standards?"

I do not doubt that I am voicing the experience of many if I say that when I first began to ask such questions I met first of all with extreme horror at such a question being put at all; and that, when I persisted, I found that it was almost entirely by women that the cost was to be borne. Women were to conform strictly to the moral standard (whose basis I was not questioning), but men need not and, generally speaking, did not. I reasoned that if men need not be chaste there must exist at least a certain number of women who *could* not be so, and that this reduced "morality" to a farce. I soon found that it was not a farce but a tragedy. These women were admittedly necessary but outcast. They were the safeguards of the rest. I wish that men would try for a moment to put themselves in the place of a young girl who learns for the first time that prostitution is the safeguard of the virtuous! I think that they would never again wonder at the rejection of such "moral standards" by the rising generation of women. You would only wonder why women had tolerated such a combination of folly and cruelty so long. You would not ask them to accept or to suffer for a "standard" like that.

Again, this morality for which (it is affirmed) society is prepared to pay so horrible a price—what is it? A physical condition! A state of body, which any man can destroy! an "honour" which lies at the mercy of a ruffian! A woman raped is a woman "dishonoured." Are her "morals" then at the mercy of another person? Is "morality" not a state of mind or of will, a spiritual passion for purity, but a material, physical thing which is only hers as long as no one snatches it from her? How senseless! How false!

When you ask a woman to-day to make the great sacrifice "in the interests of morality," you must offer her a morality that *is* moral—a morality whose justice and humanity move her to a response; not a morality which offends every instinct of justice and reality the moment the person to whom it is offered understands what it means. For what is asked to-day is too often that women should sacrifice themselves for the convenience of other people—of a hypocritical society which preaches a morality as senseless as it is base.

When older people tell me that the young seem to have "no morals at all," I ask myself whether the repudiation of much that has been called morality was not, after all, a necessity, if we are to advance at all. When I reflect on, for example, Lecky's "History of European Morals," and remember that it was not a profligate or a hedonist, but an honourable and respectable member of a civilized society, who proclaimed the prostitute the high priestess of humanity—the protectress of the purity of a thousand homes[A]—I am prepared to say that to have "no morals at all" is better than to accept such infamy and *call* it "morals"; as it is better to be an agnostic or an atheist than to worship a devil—to have no standard than to say: "Evil be thou my good."

[Footnote A: Lecky's "History of European Morals." Chap. V.]

And I believe that the tendency to reject all moral standards is largely due to the refusal of an older generation to examine and to justify its own standard. To refuse to discuss or defend it—to affirm that it is beyond debate and not to be questioned without depravity is merely to produce the impression that it is beyond defence and impossible to justify. It is not surprising that people begin to say: "Let us eat and drink, for to-morrow we die. Let us experience all we desire. Let us act like the normal healthy creatures that we are. Let us ignore the flimsy barriers a corrupt and imbecile moral code would erect between us and what we desire."

That is the point of view of many men and women to-day. That is what the absence of a just and reasoned moral code has led to. And I am prepared, in spite of all protests, to affirm that it is not a step backward, but forward; that promiscuity is not as vile as prostitution—a prostitution which has been accepted, which has been *defended* by Christian people! It is less horrible for a human being to have the morals of an animal than the morals of a devil. We have to begin by rejecting the morality of fiends, and we begin, even if the immediate effect is more terrifying to the moralist than the old hidden-up devilry that lent itself to an easier disguise.

So I believe. And so the present chaos, though it has its elements of anxiety and its obvious dangers, leaves me unafraid. I am utterly persuaded that we shall win through to solid ground.

I believe that the long groping of humanity after a sex-relationship which shall be stable, equal, passionate, disciplined, pure, is the groping of a right instinct, the hunger of a real need; and that we must—we shall—find its answer. With many failures, with many reactions, it can, I think, be seen, as history unrolls its record and civilizations rise and fall, that the movement of humanity has been towards a more stable, a more responsible, a more disciplined, but not less passionate form of relationship between men and women. Let us not forget that great and pregnant fact when we reject the immoral arguments, the cruelties and injustices, with which society has sought either to justify its ideals or to conceal its horrible failures. For if we can thus distinguish, and go forward, this generation will not have suffered in vain. It will, on the contrary, make of its suffering the spur which shall force us all onward and upward. It will by its courage and its honesty give to the world a truer and a nobler moral standard than the world has ever accepted yet.

II

A SOLUTION OF THE PROBLEM OF THE UNMARRIED

> Jesus said, "the foxes have holes, and the birds of the air
> have nests, but the Son of Man hath not where to lay his head."
> (St. Luke ix. 58.)

In the last chapter I tried to deal with the actual problem created in this country by the disproportion of the sexes—the fact that there are, roughly, one and three-quarters to two million more women than men in this country; and I was obliged to confine myself simply to stating the problem, which, to my mind, is very greatly intensified by the fact, generally ignored, that the sex needs of a woman are just as imperative, their suppression just as hard to bear, as a man's; that woman is fully as human as man, and that parenthood and loverhood and all that the satisfaction of the sex instinct means to him, it means also to her. I do not affirm that the difficulty of self-control or the suffering of abstinence presents itself to men and women in just the same way; I am sure it does not. I do not under-estimate the difference. But I do emphasize the fact that, as far as I am able to judge, the suffering is *equal*, although it is different in character. Therefore, the denial of marriage to a very large number of women means that, although some women, like some men, are naturally celibate, when so great a number of women are denied the possibility of marriage, we must take it for granted that among them the average will not be natural celibates, but women who suffer a very great loss if they do not marry.

Now I want to add that this disproportion of the sexes is quite artificial, and, therefore, should be temporary. From some of the letters I have received I gather that people imagine that there has always been a very much larger number of women than men, and not only in this country, but throughout the world; and that, therefore, we ought to shape our customs and our moral standards with this disproportion in mind as a permanent fact. I want to point out that this is not the case. The causes of the present excess of women over men in this country are quite artificial. As a matter of fact, there are more boys born in this country than girls—about 107 to 100 is the ratio—but the boys die in very much larger numbers during the first twelve months of their life, because they are more difficult to rear in bad conditions. But bad conditions are not inevitable! These babies die from preventable causes. It is not within the Providence of God that these children *must* die, nor is it a necessity of human nature. It is due to preventable causes, and is, therefore, as I say, artificial. Again, we have a very large empire, stretching out to the remoter parts of the world, and to that empire men go out in very much larger numbers than women, so that the disproportion here is, in part, the reverse side of the disproportion in the great Overseas Dominions, where there are more men than women. But that, too, is a purely artificial and temporary state of things, which has nothing to do with the fundamental conditions of human society. Finally, of course, there is the war, which again creates an artificial state of affairs, by killing enormous numbers of young men, just at the age—between twenty and forty or forty-five—when they should be growing into manhood, and becoming husbands and fathers. That again is artificial.

The reason why I emphasize this is because I feel very strongly that we must not remodel our whole society, and recreate our moral standards, to meet a passing and an artificial state of affairs. That is my answer to those who seem to think the solution of all our difficulties is to be found in the adoption of polygamy. Now polygamy is a perfectly respectable institution in a large number of countries. It is quite an old idea. It has not occurred to people for the first time between last Sunday and to-day. It has been discussed in the Sunday newspapers, which are the most widely read of any papers issued by the press. My answer to it is that such an expedient would be just an instance of this remodelling of your whole moral standard to meet an entirely artificial state of affairs. Polygamy is not possible and never has been possible on a great scale, because in hardly any country, certainly not in the world as a whole, is there a great disproportion of the sexes under ordinary circumstances. The idea most people appear to have about it is that in some parts of the world, like India and China, every man is blessed with three or four wives. It is a perfectly fantastic picture. The balance of the sexes—on the whole—is equal. It is, therefore, a physical impossibility for polygamy to be a universal custom. It cannot be practised, and has never been practised, except among the rich—a small class always. Now that surely makes it obvious that it is not a real solution. It might meet a temporary difficulty; but is it reasonable, is it statesmanlike, to alter our entire moral standard merely to tide over a temporary difficulty; to meet a state of affairs which is purely artificial? I think that morals go deeper, and should be based on some fundamental need, rather than on a purely artificial need created by a passing difficulty, however great that difficulty may be at the time. I do not, therefore, wish to dwell on other better but temporary solutions, such as emigration. I do think that this is a solution which would ease the situation to some extent, and in a normal and right way, because the disproportion in the Overseas Dominions, where the balance is the other way, and there are more men than women, is every whit as unwholesome and as disastrous as is the disproportion of women in this country. Consequently, from the point of view of both men and women, I think that emigration is a thing that ought to be considered and helped forward very much more than it is; but there, again, this is only a temporary solution. We are trying to arrive at some moral position which is based on the permanent needs and the real nature of human beings.

It has become almost a habit with me to feel that the real solution of every problem can be found, by those people who are hurt by it, if they will take hold of life *where it hurts,* and find out, not how they themselves can escape from that hurt, but how they can prevent that hurt from becoming a permanent factor in the lives of their brothers and sisters. Now, the point at which this problem hurts many of us lies in this, that women have been taught, by a curious paradox, first of all that they ought not to have any sexual feeling, any hunger, any appetite at all on that side of their natures; and secondly, that they exist solely to meet that particular physical need in men. The idea that woman was created, not like man, for the glory of God, but for the convenience of man, has greatly embittered and poisoned public opinion on this subject. Women are taught, almost from the moment they come into the world, that their chief end in existence is to be, in some way or other, a "helpmeet" for man. I remember, in the early days of the Suffrage struggle, hearing people, and women quite as often as men—more often I think—urging certain rights and principles for women, on the ground that they were meant to be the helpmeets of man. They used to quote the earlier chapters of the Book of Genesis to show that women were created for that purpose; and it was considered a very lofty kind of appeal. I think it never failed to evoke the applause of those whom you will forgive my calling a little sentimental. I do not think it ever failed to arouse in myself a deep sense of resentment. The writer of the *first* chapter of the Book of Genesis speaks of humanity as being created in the image and likeness of God, "*male and female created He them*"; there is no suggestion here that one sex was simply to be the servant of the other. That occurs in the second chapter. The idea is persistent; it is, of course, much older than the Old Testament. And it persists right into the New Testament, where you hear a man of the intellectual and spiritual calibre of St. Paul affirm that man was made for God, but woman was made for man. Down the ages this message has come, and women have been taught to consider themselves, and men to consider them, as primarily instruments of sex, of marriage and motherhood, or of other forms of serving men's needs. You do not find that feeling in Christ's attitude towards women. When people speak as though it were one of the weaknesses of Christianity that it appeals, or seems to appeal, more to women than to men, I ask you to believe that sometimes consciously, often quite unconsciously, women respond with passionate gratitude to Christ, because of His sublime teaching that every human soul was made for God, and that no part or section of society, no race, no class, and no sex, was made for the convenience of another.

I want then to combat with all my power this ancient but un-Christlike belief that women miss their object in life if they are not wives and mothers. It may seem something of a contradiction that I should in a previous chapter so have emphasized the need of women for the satisfaction of their sexual nature, and now be arguing that we must not assume that they have no right to exist if they do *not* meet this particular satisfaction; but I think you will realize that it is not a paradox when I ask you to consider for a moment what your attitude to men on this subject is. Many people hold that a man's passions are a tremendous factor in his existence, so strong that he must always be forgiven if he cannot control them; so strong that, on the whole, it is hardly to be expected that he should control them. But yet, if a man does not marry, or if there are more men than women in a certain country—as, for instance, in Australia, or Western Canada to-day—nobody speaks of those men as though they were "superfluous," as though they had ceased to have any real object for existence. People will realize that it is a hardship—a very great hardship—in their lives; they will be apt to excuse them for taking what they can get if they cannot get everything; but no human being talks of the "superfluous men" in any of our great Dominions. People always realize that a man has a *human* value, and that, however great the urgency of the sex side of him, he still is a human being, he still has his value in the world, even supposing that he should live and die celibate. If you will try to put your mind into that attitude towards women, you will, I think, see that it is not a paradox to say that a woman may and does suffer if she does not fulfil the whole of her nature, and yet that it is a monstrous fallacy to affirm that, because of that, she ceases to have any reason for existence; that she is a futile life, a person who does not really "count." Sex is a great and a mighty power, but it is something more than the mere satisfaction of a physical need. It is part of the great rhythm of life, running through all the higher creation; it is the instinct to create, going forth in the power of love, proving to us day by day that only love can create, bringing us nearer to the Divine Power, Who is Love, and Who created the heaven and the earth. In spite of our horrible thoughts about sex, our hideous sins against it, I do not think that in anything God has made man more "in His image and likeness" than when He gave him the power, through love, to create life. That is a power that makes us akin to God Himself, and the instinct of sex is not a grimy secret between two rather shamed human beings, but a great impulse of life and love—yes, even, at the height of it, an instinct to sacrifice in order that life may come into the world; it is a great bond of union between human beings; it is the secret of existence, the secret of the meaning of life; that which is to the nature of man like the sense of music to the musician, of beauty to the artist, of insight to the poet. A man may have no ear for music, and yet be a good and noble man; but who will deny that he lacks something because he has it not? A man may have no sense of beauty, but he is not, therefore, a depraved, immoral person; yet does he not stand outside some of the great secrets of life? So, when this still deeper instinct of creative love is not yours, do not congratulate yourselves, or pride yourselves that you have never felt it. For it means that you stand outside the great communion of the life of the world; it means that for you some of the music of the universe is dumb, and some of the beauty of the universe dark.

Yet how long have women been taught that this divine impulse of creation is something base! Base even in a man, belonging to his lower nature; still more deplorable in a woman, a thing to be ashamed of, a thing to crush down and suppress, a thing you would not confess to your nearest friends, or discuss with your physician. To speak of it even to your own mother would be to be met with the averted look and word of disapproval. If, as a consequence of this, women have inhibited their own nature, so that many women have created in their minds a kind of tone-deafness, a colour-blindness to this side of life, does that not seem to you a tragedy? To have so great and wonderful a thing in your nature and to suppress it as though it were something shameful and weak? Do you wonder if the term "old maid" has become synonym for everything that is narrow, and hard, and prudish and repressive? Do you wonder that the girls of this generation, confronted with the choice between such an attitude towards life as that, and its opposite—willingness to give oneself to anyone, to take all that one can get, because life refuses so much that one had hoped for—do you wonder that they often choose the second alternative? Does it seem to you so astonishing that girls, who think more than they used to, who feel that there is nothing to be ashamed of in the divine impulse of their creative womanhood, should rather take what they can get than accept that cruel, cramped attitude of sheer repression which has been all too often their only choice in the past? Is it really fair to say to them that their moral standards are going down, that they have no sense now of morality or self-respect? I tell you that if one has to make a choice between the suppression of one half —and that so beautiful a half—of human nature, and its degradation, I would not sit in judgment on those who chose either way.

But there is another possibility. You can repress, and God knows how many boys and young men, how many young women and girls have struggled to do so, and are trying to do so to-day, with a sense always of guilt and shame in their minds, laying up mental difficulties for themselves, the psychologists tell us, by this repression. You know the type; you know the kind of person who becomes hard and narrow and uncomprehending. That is one type. You can read it in their faces. The pinched look, the cramped mentality reflects itself in the body and in the face. And then there is the other type, those who have rejected this attitude towards life, denying that there is anything to be ashamed of in the natural impulse of their sex, or cause for regret if they give rein to that whose repression does so much harm, who frankly fling away the idea of self-control, because repression has seemed such a disastrous method of self-control. You can see it in their faces also; in the gradual demoralization of their nature. The rake on one hand, the prude on the other, represent the ultimate consequence of the process I am trying to describe. Many people have marked on their souls, if not on their faces, one or other of these ways of life. They have not, perhaps, gone far, they may have gone but a little way in one direction or the other; but the mark on the soul remains all the same. And when you see the extreme result, the prude on one side, the rake on the other, do you not begin to desire a better way? To ask yourself whether there is not a third choice before you?

I believe there is; and the choice is this: It is neither the repression nor the degradation, but *transformation* of the sex side of our nature. I will take as the supreme example of that transformation the figure of Christ Himself—Christ who had neither wife nor child—St. Francis of Assisi, St. Catherine of Siena, St. Theresa of Spain. Four of the greatest figures—One of them supreme—who were not "natural celibates" in the sense that implies that they did not have surging through them the divine impulse of creative love; for these are the greatest lovers the world has ever seen, and compared with theirs even the great love of one man for one woman, one woman for one man, is the lesser thing. But these great figures in human history are those on whose hearts Humanity itself made such a claim that it became impossible for them to give to one what was claimed by all the world. You will see that this is not a denial of creative love, for no one in the world has so loved the world as these. They are the beacons of humanity in this matter of love, and how are they, shall we say, how are they not fathers and mothers, whose spiritual children are all over the world? Have they not born into the world with travail of soul, the souls of men and women? These great Lovers of Humanity were not lacking in passion; had they been they could not have moved the world; but their passion was transmuted to the service of Humanity itself, for nothing else was great or wide enough for such a love. Does anyone suppose that it was a mere instinct of asceticism that drove St. Francis to make out of snow, cold images of wife and child? Was it not rather the sudden resurgent desire of the greatest of the saints for some more humanly warm affection, something more individual, something that nestles more closely to the heart, than this great service of Humanity? And in a savage irony he mocks his pain. "There are thy children, there is thy wife," says St. Francis, and his cry is not the answer of the spirit to a lustful temptation: it was the cry of a lonely human heart for the human happiness of wife and children and home. Aye, and I would claim that Our Lord Himself had this desire. For I cannot doubt that in that glorious young manhood of His, so full of power and sympathy and love, this agony of longing sometimes swept over Him. He whose vitality and power were such that He hardly knew fatigue, who was so close a friend, so much loved and sought by women, so tender to little children, so young, so strong—is it not certain that He was indeed "tempted in all things like as we are"? How could one so physically vital, so humanly and divinely full of love, escape the conflict? That He conquered we know; that He suffered we cannot doubt. All His perfect humanity speaks to us in that lonely cry: "The foxes have holes, and the birds of the air have nests, but the Son of Man hath not where to lay His head." Do not dream, those of you who may have to struggle with your own nature, do not dream that Christ has not been there with you, that He had nothing to feel or to suffer. How would He have developed that spiritual power, how would He have become so great a Lover of the world if He knew nothing of that side of life? But He, and His greatest followers—St. Francis of Assisi, St. Catherine and St. Theresa, and countless others who have followed them—learned to transmute that great creative force, disdained both choices which I set before you, finding a nobler and more glorious way. These would neither repress this great impulse, nor dissipate it, but so used it for the service of man that there is in all the history of man no life more rich, more human, more full of love, more full of creation, or more full of power, than the lives of these celibate men and women, who learned from Christ how they could live and love.

It is not easy for men and women this way, but it is possible. It is possible, and it is glorious; and, in its degree, the need for it comes to everyone. Do not imagine that it is not needed in marriage as well as out of marriage. Every married lover will tell you that if his love is to remain what it was in the beginning—if it is rather to grow in power and beauty—he also must be able gradually to transmute his love in such a way that the spirit dominates the flesh more and more, and that the physical side of marriage becomes simply an expression of the love of the spirit, the perfect final expression, the sacrament of love. Do not imagine that this is not needed, this effort, and this power, by every human being who desires to be human in his love, and not something less than human. And to those to whom the need comes in its sternest form, I will not pretend for a moment that it is not hard. Nay, I will prophesy to you that if you do so choose to serve the world, it will to all of you sometimes seem too hard. With Christ, with St. Francis, your human nature will sometimes assert itself. "The foxes have holes, and the birds of the air have nests, but the Son of Man"—the

Servant of Humanity—has no such joy. But of whatever life you choose, that is sometimes true. To the finest spirit in marriage there comes sometimes the thought that, but for this great claim, he might have undertaken some adventure, might have answered some call, which now he cannot answer. Does that mean that he regrets his choice? No, not for a moment! It only means that human nature is so rich and so varied that whatever life you forego will sometimes seem to you the better choice. You will think, for a moment, that you might have chosen differently. If that happened to St. Francis, believe me, it will happen to you. But yet, is it not a heroic path that I point out to you? Is it not possible that to this generation heroism may be possible in such a way, on such a scale, that you will leave this world nobler in moral stature because of the hardness which you endured, the choice that you made? Women, to whom this comes home specially at this time, may it not be that you, by taking this way, will become the mothers in spirit of women in a happier generation, on whom will never again be imposed our cramped, stifling, sub-human conception of what women ought to be? You will show to the world not only that the individual woman of genius may have a value to Humanity beyond her sex, but that every woman has that value. In solving your own problem, and taking hold of life where most it hurts you, you will end by making a moral standard nobler, a humanity richer and more human, a womanhood freer, greater, more Christlike than it was. And future generations shall rise up and call you blessed.

III

CONSIDERATION OF OTHER SOLUTIONS OF THE PROBLEM OF THE DISPROPORTION OF THE SEXES

> "My spirit's bark is driven
> Far from the shore, far from the trembling throng
> Whose sails were never to the tempest given."

Shelley: "Adonais."

Let us now move away from that aspect of the moral problem which has concerned us hitherto—that of the difficulties created by the disproportion of the sexes at this time and in this country—and consider the problem as it presents itself under more normal conditions. For even in ages and in countries where there are an equal number of men and women there are difficulties in their relations with one another, and a "moral problem."

People ask, for example, whether sex-relationships should be governed by law at all; whether they should continue in any given case when passion has died, or when love (which is more than passion) has gone. Should love ever be other than perfectly free, and is not the attempt to bind it essentially "immoral"? Should it ever be exclusive or proprietary? Is not the "moral problem" really created, not by human nature, but by the attempt to bind what cannot be bound and to coerce what should be free?

The answer given to such questions is often to-day on the side of what is called, mistakenly, I think, "free love." And in considering this answer, I want to remind you that it is often given by people who are most sincere, most idealistic, in their own lives and in their own love. Indeed it has often been pointed out that it is at times of great spiritual exaltation and fervour that the cult of "free love" is most likely to find adherents. The great principle that "love is the fulfilling of the law" is held with a fervour which makes any question as to what love is, and how much it involves, seem half-hearted and cold. Those who preach this doctrine remind us—and very justly—of the weakness and insincerity of the "orthodox" moral standard, whether it is enforced by law or by custom. They revolt against the proprietary and possessive view of marriage as giving a woman "a hold over her husband" when he has "grown tired of her," or as justifying a man in enforcing upon his wife the rights which only love makes right, when she has grown tired of him. I appeal, therefore, to those to whom the dispassionate discussion of "free love" seems quite outrageous, to remember that there are those to whom this teaching is *not* a mere excuse for licence, but an attempt to reach something lovelier and nobler than the present moral code, whose failures and insincerities no thinking person can ignore.

In considering this view, I want first to point out that although to have no legal or enforceable tie in sex-relationships seems on the surface much the simplest and easiest way to arrange life, although permanent monogamous marriage is exceedingly difficult and inconvenient, yet the movement of humanity does seem to have been on the whole in that direction. It is, of course, untrue to say that among primitive peoples there is anything that can fairly be called promiscuity. Historians and anthropologists have taught us that among all peoples, however barbarous, there are conventions, sanctions, tabus, by which the relations of men and women are regulated. The customs of such people may seem to us mere licence; but they are not so. And some of the customs of more "civilized" countries are at least as horrifying to the "savage" as his can be to us. Nevertheless, it is true to say that as civilization advances, and especially where the position of women improves, the movement has been towards a more stable and exclusive form of marriage. We grope uncertainly towards it: we fail atrociously. Yet we do not abandon an ideal which asks so much of human nature that human nature is continually invoked to prove its impossibility.

Why have we persisted? It is idle to speak of monogamy as though it were a senseless rule imposed on unfortunate humanity by some all-powerful Superman. We have imposed it on ourselves. It is our doing. Why have we done it? Surely because, in spite of its alleged "impossibility," its obvious inconveniences, there is some need in human nature which demands a permanent and a stable sex relationship to meet it.

I believe that there is something in our human nature which desires stability in its relations with other human beings. It is perhaps a recognition of the fact that, though we live in time and suffer its conditions, we are immortal also and chafe under too strict a bondage to time. Our relations with other human beings ought not to be evanescent! There is something cheap and shoddy in the giving and taking of human personality on such easy soon-forgotten terms. It is not only in sexual relations that this is true. It is true of all human intercourse. The longer care and devotion of human parents for their offspring is not a physical only, but a spiritual necessity: and it is bound up with the greater faithfulness of human lovers. In parenthood, in loverhood, in friendship, those who take their obligations lightly are not the finer sort of men and women, but the slighter, cheaper make. It is not a love of freedom but a certain inferiority and shoddiness that makes it possible for us to give ourselves, and take others, lightly. For in all human relationships it is "ourselves" that we give and take. It is not what your friend does for you or gives to you that makes him your friend; but what he *is* to you. It is his personality that you have shared. And so there is something rather repulsive in quickly forgetting or throwing it away. People who make friends and lose them as the trees put out their leaves in spring to shed them in the autumn, are not quite human. The capacity to make friends—to make many friends—is a great power: the capacity to lose them not so admirable. Yet there are people who always have a bosom-friend, every time you meet them; only it is never the same friend. And this is a poor sort of friendship, for it *is* poor to give and take so little that you easily cease or forget to give at all.

If this is true of friends, it is not less true of lovers: it is more true. For sex-love includes more of one's personality, it more completely involves body, soul and spirit, is the most perfect form of union that human beings know. How strange, then, to argue that one may treat a lover as one would not treat a friend! Make one and lose one so lightly, and disavow all the responsibility of a love in which so much is given, so much involved! It is true that all human love has a physical element, even if it is only the desire for the physical presence of the beloved one. We all want sometimes to see and to touch our friends. But in sex-love that physical element becomes a desire for perfect union, expressing a spiritual harmony. Can one take such a gift lightly, and pass from one relationship to another with a readiness which would seem contemptible in a friend?

It is this holding of human personality cheap that is really immoral, really dishonest: for it is not cheap. It is this which makes prostitution a horror, and prostitutes the Ishmaels of their race. They "sell cheap what is most dear," and, knowing this, rage against their buyers. The hideously demoralizing effect of a life of prostitution on the soul is a commonplace. "These women," it has been said, "sink so low that they cease to know what love is, they cease to be able to give. They can only cheat and steal and sell." It is true. Whatever virtues of kindliness and pity the prostitute may (and often does) have for other unfortunates and outcasts, her attitude in general does become that of the parasite, the swindler, the vampire. Why? Because on her the deepest outrage against human personality is committed. Without a shadow of claim, without a pretence of offering its equivalent, that, in her, is bought and sold which is beyond price. Why should she not cheat and thieve? Take all she can, she cannot get the true value of what has been bought from her. Does she reason all that out? More often than we think. But whether she reasons consciously or not, she knows she has been defrauded: and she defrauds.

But it is the buying and selling, I shall be told, that makes her so vile: between such a sale and the free gift of lovers lies the whole difference between morality and immorality. I do not think so. It is the contemptuous use of another which is immoral, and though actually to buy and sell the person is the lowest depth of immorality, because it is the lowest and most brutal expression of such contempt, any lightness or irreverence is "immoral" in its degree; so therefore is conduct which makes love an evanescent thing, or the giving of personality which love involves, a passing emotion.

If we feel this to be so in friendship, surely it is more and not less true of a union so complete on every plane as that of sex. Can you take that—and give it—and pass on, as though it were a light thing?

The desire for permanence, for stability, for trustworthiness lies very deep in human nature. We may—we do—rebel against it, and speak with rapture of an unfettered existence without material ties: but even in material things the nomad is the least creative, the least civilized of his kind. His existence is neither so picturesque nor so human as we imagine. One has only to read history to see how little he has contributed to humanity—and how little he has helped to raise the human level above the animal. It is not for nothing that we find the home imposed upon human kind by the necessities of human infancy. It is the helplessness of the child that has humanized our species by creating the home which its helplessness demanded, and though a great deal that is sentimental is said about homes, this remains a fact. The nomadic, the homeless race gives little to the world; it is by nature and circumstances an exploiter of resources for which it feels no responsibility, from which it is content to take without giving. Reading in a pamphlet of Professor Toynbee's the other day, I found this description of the Eastern world in the 15th and 16th centuries of our era:—"Even when the East began to recover and comparatively stable Moslem states arose again in Turkey and Persia and Hindustan, *the nomadic taint was in them and condemned them to sterility*…. One gets the impression not of a government administering a country, but of *a horde of nomads exploiting it*."[B]

[Footnote B: The italics are mine.—A.M.R.]

Even so is it with human love. These nomads of the affections give and take so little as they pass from hand to hand that they become cheap and have little left to give at last: nor do they really get what they would take. Men and women claim the right to "experience," but experience of what? We do not live by bread alone, and the physical experience is not really all we seek. It is something, however? Yes—certainly something: but by a paradox familiar enough in human affairs, to snatch the lesser is to sacrifice the greater. The experimental lover, the giver whose small and careful gift is for a time, claims in the name of "experience," of the "fulfilment of his nature," what really belongs only to a greater giving. Such lovers are like a rich man who sets out tramping with nothing in his pocket. He may suffer temporary inconvenience, but is within safe distance of his banking account. He plays with a risk he can never really know, since knowledge and experience are not for those "whose sails were never to the tempest given." The prudent lover whose love is lightly given for as long as it lasts is as wise—and as futile.

I think, too, that those who offer this little price for so great a thing have nothing left at last. To taste love, to *use* the great passion of sex is on a par with the exploitation of genius on a series of "pot-boilers." Genius may outlast a few such meannesses, but they will murder it at last, and the man who by pot-boiling has gained the opportunity to create a real work of art finds there is no more art left in him. He has now the leisure, the opportunity, the public: but not the power. So is it with those who lightly use so great a thing as sex. Yielded to every impulse, given to each "new-hatched, unfledged companion," it loses its capacity for greatness, and the experience desired passes for ever from the grasp.

It is this which, to my mind, rules out the "experimental marriage." Much may be said for it—and has been, and is being said by people whose judgment must command respect. But love is impatient of lending. If it is not given outright in the belief that the gift is final, can the "experiment" be valid? Is not this very sense of finality—this desire to give and burn one's ships—of the very essence of love? One cannot experiment in finality.

It is true that many marriages would not have taken place, and had much better not have taken place, if there had been greater knowledge: but we have yet to learn what greater knowledge can do even without experiment. Hitherto we have gone to the opposite extreme and buried all that belongs to sex not in a fog of ignorance only, but under a mountain of hypocrisy and lies. Let in the light, and see if we cannot do better! And though it is true that some things cannot be known by any amount of teaching, and wait upon experience, yet I submit that the essential experience is realized only when it is believed to be the expression of an undying love—a gift and not a loan.

Let me say one last word on the solution to our moral difficulties proposed by those who affirm for every woman "the right to motherhood." This claim is based on the belief that the creative impulse is more, or more consciously, present in the sexual nature of a woman than of a man, and that, in consequence, the satisfaction of that impulse is to a great extent the satisfaction of a need which makes the disproportionate number of women in any country a real tragedy. It is impossible to generalize with any degree of confidence about the sexual nature of either man or woman in our present state of crude and barbarous ignorance; but I am inclined—very tentatively—to agree that this generalization is correct, and that the creative impulse is an even stronger factor in the sexual life of women than of men. I realize the cruelty of a civilization in which war and its accessories create an artificial excess of women over men, and in consequence deprive hundreds of thousands of women of motherhood. I do not think I underestimate that cruelty or its tragic consequences. I admit the "right" of women to the exercise of their vocation and the fulfilment of their nature.

But I affirm that those who base upon this claim the right to bring children into the world, where society has made marriage impossible, are not moved to do so by the instinct of motherhood. No, no, for motherhood is more than a physical act; it is a spiritual power. Its first thought is not for the right of the mother but of the child. And what are a child's rights? A home—two parents—all that makes complete the spiritual as well as the material meaning of "home." I do not believe that there is any woman who is the mother of young children, and a widow, who does not daily realize how irreparable is the loss sustained by the fatherless. War perhaps has inflicted that loss upon them; it is one of the iniquities of war. And though the mother tries all she can—yes, and works miracles of love to make herself all she *can* be to her child, that loss cannot wholly be made up. I speak with intensity of conviction on this point, for I have myself a little adopted child—orphaned of both parents—in my home. I never see other children with their parents without realizing what she has lost not only in her mother but her father. There is needed the different point of view, the different relationship, bringing with it a fuller and a richer experience of life. What woman that hast lost her husband does not realize the truth of what I say?

It is beside the mark to say that a bad father is worse than no father, or

And then human beings are three-fold in nature. They have a body, a mind—or what St. Paul calls a "soul"—and a spirit. "Soul" is a word whose meaning we have altered so much that I must define what I mean by it and what I think St. Paul meant by it. The soul includes the emotions and the intellect, that part of a man which is not wholly physical and which is not entirely spiritual. Everyone has a soul. And every one of you, however much you ignore your body, however much you may tell me your body does not really exist, have got a body too. You have to eat and drink and sleep, just like the most material alderman, though you may eat less. And you cannot base a real moral standard on the pretence that you have not got a body. You are, on one side of your nature, physical, material, animal; but you have got a mind and emotions or "soul"; and you have got a spirit. To act as though you had not is just as futile as to pretend that you have not got a body. "Where there is no vision the people perish." "Mankind is incurably religious." "All the world seeks after God." Those proverbs, those sayings, which are familiar to all, crystallize the world's experience that human beings are spiritual beings. If there is any person who thinks that he is merely an intellect and a body, I will direct the attention of that intellect of his away from himself to the race, and I will remind him that practically no race in the world has ever been entirely without the sense of God; that, however hard men try, they have never been able to cure humanity of its spiritual hunger; that though our gods are often gross and earthy, even diabolical, yet they are spiritual, and they are the proof that man is spiritually aware; that he is a spirit as well as a body and a soul. Now I say that anyone who tries to base his morality on the assumption that he is only a body, or only an intelligence, or only a spirit, has got a false standard, and his morality is a dishonest kind of morality. The body will avenge itself on those who ignore it. Psychologists are teaching us that the mind will avenge itself on those who ignore it. And this is just as true of the spirit. Where there is no vision the people do perish. Your spiritual nature avenges itself on those who try to rule it out. Base your morality either on the exclusion of any part of your being, or on the assumption that what you do concerns yourself alone; and you will find that you are violating human nature. It is useless for you to act wrongly and to affirm that you do it "because human nature is what it is." When you do so, you are assuming that human nature is *not* what it is; that is to say you assume that it is purely physical, when, in fact, it is three-fold—body, soul and spirit. You can see for yourselves, I think, how this violation of human nature works itself out. For animals promiscuity is not wrong. When they treat themselves as purely animals they are basing their moral standard, if I may put it so, on bed-rock; they *are* animals, and therefore they behave as animals without violating any law of their being. As they rise higher in the scale of evolution their morals become nobler. There are moral standards among the lower animals, but they remain at a certain level, and rightly so. No animal is harmed by behaving like an animal, for in doing so he obeys the law of his being; but if human beings behave as though they were animals, what happens? They find to their horror that they have let loose upon the world detestable, hideous and devastating diseases. Do you think that medicine will ever be able to rid the world of what are called the diseases of immorality as long as immorality remains? I do not believe it. I know that you can do much for individual sufferers, though you cannot do one-tenth part of what doctors thought they were going to be able to do, eight or nine years ago. And, of course, whatever we can do, we must and ought to do. But we do not reach the root of the matter by medicine.

No scientist can tell us how small-pox or tuberculosis or rheumatism first entered the world; but any scientist can tell us that by wrong living, wrong housing, wrong feeding, we can breed and spread and perpetuate disease. In other words, we are diseased not because we obey the laws of our nature but because we violate them: and though we can take the individual sufferer and (sometimes) cure him, we shall not get rid of the disease until we have learnt to obey those laws and to live rightly.

In just the same way the diseases of vice, though no one can say how they first came into the world, continue and flourish, not because of human nature, but because we violate some law of our own nature in what we do. We may even cure the individual; we may see a thousand struck and a thousand guilty escape; the fact remains that these diseases are bred in the swamp of immorality, just as certainly as malaria is bred in the mosquito-haunted pools of the malaria swamp. Drain the swamp, and you get rid of the malaria, for there is no longer any place for the malaria-bearing mosquito to breed. Drain the swamp of immorality, and you get rid of venereal disease, because there is no longer a place where these diseases can breed. Live rightly, and your nature will respond in health. When human beings elect to make their relations with one another promiscuous—when, that is to say, they treat themselves as animals—they are not obeying, they are violating the law of their own being; for they are not animals only, and to treat themselves as such is to disobey the law of their own nature. And disobedience reacts in disease.

So again, the relations of men and women are of the mind as well as of the body and the spirit. You cannot rule out your mind, and I think that those who believe, as many do today, not indeed in a merely animal promiscuity, but in rather casual relations between men and women—experiments, if you like, men and women passing from one union to another—rule out the fact that a human being has a mind, a memory and foresight; that our being includes a past, and, in a sense, includes a future also; and when you try to divorce your physical experience from your intellectual and emotional being you are again violating the law of your own nature.

I remember asking one of the most happily married women that I know to put into words, if she could, the reason why she believed that married people, married lovers, should not have gone through other relationships with other people before they gave themselves to one another. I asked her to express in words what seemed to her immoral. She wrote this: "In the ideal union between God and man, we know that man must give the fulness of his being, body, mind and spirit, throughout his whole life, to God, and that anything less than this, though it may be fine and noble, does fall short of perfection. It is the same with the human love of men and women. The 'fulness of our being' which we desire to give to our lover consists not only in what we are at any given moment but in what we have been in the past, what we may become in the future. And so in the formation of merely temporary unions the highest and deepest unity can never be fully achieved." She went on to say: "When we have passed beyond the physical sphere we shall be able, like God, to give ourselves equally to all; but while we are in the flesh we cannot share ourselves equally with all, and any attempt to do so lowers the standard of perfect human love." I like that, because it is based again on a loyal acceptance of human nature. We are not yet as God in the sense that, being wholly spirit, we can share ourselves equally with all. We do still live in bodies, and we have in this life memory and prevision, and surely that is indeed an ideal union, if we are looking for the highest, which is able to give its past and its future as well as its present, so that the whole personality is involved, in that act of union, and that anything short of that is at least not quite perfect. Human beings are still in the body, and are yet soul and spirit in that body, and must take both into account. Divorce the physical from the spiritual in yourself, and you are violating yourself. Divorce the physical from the spiritual in someone else —you who perhaps say: "I myself love such a man, such a woman, with the best part of myself; what I do with another is of no importance"—you violate the nature of that other from whom you take what is physical, and leave what is spiritual as though it were not there.

Your life, like your body, is too highly organized, too sensitive, too knit together by memories and prevision for you to leave behind you anything that has really entered into your life. It is a shoddy and superficial nature that passes easily from experience to experience, and when you look at such you can see how shallower still it becomes. It is the deeper and the loftier nature that cannot enter into any human relationship and then pass away from it altogether unchanged. And even that shoddy, that poor, that mean little soul which seems to pass so lightly from one experience to another does not really altogether escape. Some mark is left upon the soul, some association remains in the memory; and again and again marriages have been wrecked because a man has taken the associations of the gutter into the sanctuary of his home. Unwillingly, with an imagination that fain would reject the stain, he has injured, he has insulted the love that has now come to him, the most precious thing on earth, because he has not known how to do otherwise; because all the associations of passion have been to him degraded, smirched, treated frivolously in the past. It is true of men; it is also true of women. I do not know of anything that makes understanding harder between two people than the fact that one has had experiences and associations which the other has not had and does not understand, because they are on an entirely different level. These create between them, with all the desire for understanding in the world, a barrier of misunderstanding and incomprehension, which is all the more fatal because it is so intangible, so obscure, so hard to put into words, so often actually unconscious or subconscious in the mind of one or of the other.

Again, you must not think that you are altogether spirit, and here perhaps it is the woman who is more apt to sin than the man. How often have I talked to women who speak of the physical side of love as though it were something base and unworthy! Such a conception of passion is inhuman, and therefore it is not really moral. A woman who thinks of this sacrament of love, for which perhaps the man who loves her has kept himself clean all his life, as a base thing, and who treats it as though it were a concession to something base in a man's nature, instead of being the very consecration of body and soul at once, the sacrament of union, one of the loveliest things in human nature—such a woman gives as great a shock to what is sacred and lovely in her husband's nature as he when he brings with him into his marriage the associations of the street. It is as hard, it is as insulting, it makes marriage as difficult in understanding, one way as the other. For it is not true that our bodies are vile and base; they are the temples of the Holy Spirit.

Or if you think that you can stand alone, that what you do is the concern of no one else, that your life is a solitary thing, so solitary that no man or woman is concerned, no one but yourself, and you may sin alone—there again you misunderstand. You cannot stand alone, and nothing that you say or think or do leaves the world unchanged. Is that difficult to believe in these days, when psychology is teaching us how all-important thought is? Ought you to find it hard to believe that what you do in the utmost secrecy affects others, since it affects you, and no man lives to himself alone? I do not wish to exaggerate. I have a horror of those books and people who speak in exaggerated terms of any kind of sexual lapse. I am persuaded that human beings can rise from such mistakes, and rise much more easily than from the subtler spiritual sins which have so much more respectable an air. But yet do not sin under the impression that what you do concerns yourself alone. Do not use, for your own satisfaction only, powers which were given you for creation and for the world.

But this, you may say, is not the accepted standard of morality. That is a matter rather of laws and ceremonies. And people begin to ask; "What real difference can a mere ceremony make?" It does not make any difference to the morality of your relationships with your fellow men and women. Nothing that is immoral becomes moral because it has been done under a legal contract, or consecrated by a rite. There, I think, is where the world has gone so wrong. The idea that a relation that is selfish, cruel, mercenary, becomes moral because someone has said some words over you, and you have signed a register—what a farcical idea! How on earth does that change anything at all? The morality of all civil or religious ceremony lies, I think, in this—that by accepting and going through it, you accept the fact that your love does concern others besides yourself; it will concern your children; and beyond that, it concerns the world. You are right when you ask your friends to come and rejoice with you at your wedding. It is the concern of all the world when people love each other, and it is the failure of *love* that concerns them when marriage is a failure. Such failure chills the atmosphere; it shakes our faith in love as the supreme power in the universe; it makes us all waver in our allegiance to constancy and love when love fails. It is a joyful thing when people love. "All the world loves a lover." It is an old saying, but what a true one! It *is* our concern when people nobly and loyally love each other, it is the concern of the community, and those who take upon themselves these public vows seem to me to have a more truly moral conception of love than those who say: "This is our affair only; it is not the affair of the State or the affair of the Church." But the actual ceremony must be the expression of a moral feeling such as that. It cannot in itself make moral what is immoral! The old idea that if a woman was seduced by a man she was "made honest" by the man marrying her is essentially immoral. Very likely all that she knew about the man was that she could not trust him, and to suppose that we can set right what is wrong by tying them together for the rest of their lives is to imagine an absurdity and to establish a lie.

Or take the case from another point of view. I have two in my mind at this moment, who for some reason (a reason not very far to seek if you read our English marriage laws) came to the conclusion that it is not right to place oneself in such a position as a married woman is in under English law. I am not discussing whether they were right or wrong; I say that quite sincere and moral people do come to that conclusion sometimes, and so did these two. They lived together, therefore, without being legally married. They were absolutely faithful to each other; their love was as responsible, as dignified, as true as any such relation could be. It lacked to my mind one thing—the sense of a wider responsibility—but then it had very much that many legal marriages have not. Those two people are put outside society; it is made almost impossible for them to earn their living; and at last in despair they go to the registry office, and sign their names in a book. What difference has been made in their relation to each other? Absolutely none. They are no more convinced of the right and duty of the community to be concerned with marriage than they were before. They have yielded to coercion. Their moral standard, good or bad, is precisely what it was; their relation to each other wholly unchanged. But in the eyes of the world they have become respectable, they are "moral," they can be received back into the bosom of society. And why? Because they have gone through a ceremony in which they do not believe!

Every marriage in the world probably lacks something of perfection. There are no perfect human beings, and, therefore, hardly, perhaps, a perfect marriage; and to my mind those who do not admit the concern of the community in their marriage do lack something. But to suppose that those people are immoral, when others who live together, legally licensed to do so, in selfishness, in infidelity, for financial reasons, or for social reasons, are moral is fundamentally dishonest. When a woman sells her body for money, do you think that it makes it moral that she does it in a church or in a registry office? Is there one whit of difference, morally, between the prostitution that has no legal recognition and the prostitution that has? Is it anything but prostitution to sell yourself for money, whether you are a man or a woman? Do you imagine that because you have a contract to protect you while you do it, you are doing what is moral? If you marry for any reason but love—for experience, to "complete your nature"—without much regard to the man or woman you marry, or to the children you bring into the world, are you not exploiting human nature just as certainly, though not so brutally, as a man who buys a woman in the street? It is not so base a form of exploitation, God knows; that I admit; but when there is *any* element of exploitation in the bargain it is not made more truly moral because it happens to be blessed in a church or registered in an office. The legal ceremony must be the outcome of a morality which makes you realize that what you do affects other people, that what you do most profoundly affects the children that you hope to have, and that the community has both an interest and a responsibility in all this. That is "moral." But if the relationship thus to be legalized is not moral, it is dishonest to pretend that it can be made so by any ceremony which those concerned may undergo.

But, you will say, we cannot peer into other people's lives and judge them in this kind of way. How are we to know? How are we, who have many friends, many neighbours, on whom our standards must react, to judge their lives? We can tell who has gone through a legal ceremony and who refuses to do so. That is a nice convenient rule by which we can judge and condemn such people. But we cannot go poking into people's lives and studying their motives and judging their fundamental moral standards! No, you cannot. Why should you? This little set of iron rules makes it very easy to judge, does it not? But why do you desire it to be easy to judge? You and I know how infinite are the gradations between the most noble kind of chastity and the most ignoble kind of immorality; but which of us is to create a rigid standard and measure our friends and acquaintances against it? We do not do it with the other virtues: why do we desire to do it with this one? Take such a virtue as truth. Conceive the crystalline sincerity of some truth-loving minds, realize that some have such a devotion to truth that the faintest shadow of insincerity—not a lie, but the merest shadow of insincerity in the depths of their hearts—is abhorrent to them. Consider the infinite gradations between that mind and the mind which takes a lie for truth, a mind that is rotten with corruption, that does not know how to think straight, let alone care to speak straight. You do not draw up your little set of rules and say: "I do not call on that person because he does not speak the truth; and I won't have anything to do with that one—such persons are outside the social pale altogether because their conception of truth is different from mine!"

No, you keep your admiration for the truth-loving and the sincere. You recognize that people have different standards about what is truth. One person will never tell a lie under any circumstances: another will reckon himself free to tell a lie to save a third, or to preserve a confidence; will you judge which is the more honourable of the two? Where is your little set of rules? You cannot have one. You shrink from the person who is morally dishonest and corrupt; you worship the person who loves truth as Darwin loved it. But between those two extremes what an infinite variety of attainment! Who can say: "These people are moral because they are married, and those are immoral, they are not married?" It is not true, it is not honest, to make these rules our measure. They do not meet the realities of human nature, and I contend that we, who have known souls so chaste and lovely that they make us in love with virtue, do far more to raise the moral standard of humanity by seeking to imitate such people than by setting up our little codes of rules and condemning or justifying all men by them. Let us treat this virtue as we do every other virtue, not fitting it to a set of rules which everyone knows do not fit the realities, but taking our courage in our hands and judging human beings (if we must judge them) by their real sincerity, their real unselfishness, their real unwillingness to exploit others—the measure of the chastity of their souls.

V

THE MORAL STANDARD OF THE FUTURE: WHAT SHOULD IT BE?

"Ye have heard that it was said by them of old time, Thou shalt not commit adultery: but I say unto you, That whosoever looketh on a woman to lust after her hath committed adultery with her already in his heart. It hath been said, Whosoever shall put away his wife let him give her a writing of divorcement: But I say unto you that whosoever shall put away his wife, saving for the cause of fornication, causeth her to commit adultery: and whosoever shall marry her that is divorced committeth adultery.

"Again ye have heard that it has been said by them of old time, Thou shalt not forswear thyself, but shall perform unto the Lord thine oaths: but I say unto you, Swear not at all; neither by heaven; for it is God's throne; nor by the earth; for it is his footstool; neither by Jerusalem; for it is the city of the great King. Neither shalt thou swear by thy head, because thou canst not make one hair white or black. But let your communications be, Yea, yea; Nay, nay: for whatsoever is more than these cometh from evil." (Matthew v., 27-28; 31-37.)

I have tried to reach those realities of human nature on which human morality must be based. I believe that the fundamental things which we must take into account are, first, the complex nature of human beings, who having body, soul, and spirit to reckon with cannot neglect any one of these without insincerity; and, secondly, the solidarity of the human race, which makes it futile to act as though the "morals" of any one of us could be his own affair alone.

It is because of this solidarity that marriage has always been regarded as a matter of public interest, to be recognized by law, celebrated by some public ceremony, protected by a legal contract. All are concerned in this matter, for it affects the race itself, through the children that may be born.

Human children need what animals do not, or not to the same extent. They need two parents: they need a stable and permanent home: they need a spiritual marriage, a real harmony between their parents, as well as a physical one. A child is not provided for when you have given it a home and food and clothing, since it is a spirit as well as a body—a soul and a spirit, a being craving for love, and needing to live in an atmosphere of love. The young of no other species need this as children do, and therefore, it is the concern of the community to see that the rights of these most helpless and most precious little ones are safeguarded. I cannot believe that any State calling itself civilized can ever disregard the duty of safeguarding the human rights of the child, and I repeat its human rights are not sufficiently met when its physical necessities are guaranteed. But I go further. I claim that it is really the concern of all of us that people who love should do so honestly, faithfully, responsibly. Marriage should be permanent; that is true in a sense that makes it important to all of us that it should succeed. Those who have loved and ceased to love have not failed for themselves only but for all. They have shaken the faith of the world. They have inclined us to the false belief that love is not eternal. They have, so far as they could, destroyed a great ideal, injured a great faith. People—and some of these are my personal friends, and people for whom I have a very great respect—who affirm that a legal or religious marriage is not necessary because their relations to one another are not the concern of the community, may have, it seems to me, a morality that is lofty, but not one that is broad, not one that is truly human. It is not true (and, therefore, it is not moral) to say that marriage is not the concern of other people. No one can fail in love, no one can take on himself so great a responsibility and fail to fulfil it, without all of us being concerned. Humanity is *solidaire*. The community is and must be concerned in the love of men and women in marriage. But what should be the nature of that concern? What should we—the community—hold up as the right standard of sex-relationship, and what methods should we use to impose it on others? I think you will have gathered from what I have said already that, to my mind, marriage should be a union that looks forward to being permanent, faithful, monogamous. It should be the expression of a union of spirit so perfect that the union of the bodies of those who love follows as a kind of natural necessity. It should be the sacrament of love, "the outward and visible sign of an inward and spiritual grace." And something of this perfection is to be found in many marriages that seem (and are) far from complete. I often hear of the lives of married people where there has been very much to overcome, where perhaps the marriage has been entered into in ignorance and error; where the passion that brought the two together has been very evanescent; where it has soon become evident that their temperaments do not "fit"; where it might easily be said that they were not really "married" at all: yet there has been in these two such a stubborn loyalty to responsibilities undertaken, such a magnificent sense of faithfulness, such a determination to make the best out of what they have rather lightly undertaken; sometimes even only on one side, there has been such faith, such honour, such loyalty, such a refusal to admit a final failure, that a relationship poor in promise has become beautiful and sacred. In face of such loyalty, the theory that sex-relationships can rightly be brief, evanescent, thrown aside as soon as passion has gone, seems to me very cheap and shoddy, very unworthy of human beings. Marriage should be all that—shall I say?—the Brownings made of it. But when it is not, there is still often much that is left. Men and women, you cannot enter into one another's lives in this deep and intimate way and go on your way as though nothing had happened. You cannot tear asunder people so united without bleeding. You cannot make a failure of it without immeasurable loss.

"How do I love thee? Let me count the ways.
I love thee to the depth and breadth and height
My soul can reach, when feeling out of sight
For the ends of Being and ideal Grace.
I love thee to the level of everyday's
Most quiet need, by sun and candlelight."

Who that has once heard this can easily take anything less? Or who, having loved in any of these ways, will lightly break the bond? I think that one of the most profoundly moral relationships I have ever met between a man and a woman was, in spite of all that I have said up till now, the relationship of a man to a woman to whom at first he was not legally married. It was her wish, not his, but they were not legally married. They had no children, and she was unfaithful to him more than once, and yet this man—and he did not call himself a Christian—this man felt that he had taken the responsibility of that woman's life, and though he could easily have put her away, and though, at last, she killed in him all that you would normally call love between a man and woman, and he learned to care for another woman, yet he would not abandon her because now she had grown to need him, and he felt he could not take so great a human responsibility as the life of another person and then cast it away as though it had never been.

That is morality. To such a sense of what human relationships demand my whole soul gives homage. That seems to me a perfectly humane and, therefore, truly moral idea of what love involves. Such a sense of responsibility should go with all love. Passion cannot last, in the nature of things, and, therefore, those who marry do so, if they know anything at all of love—and, God help them, many of them do not—but if they know anything at all of love, they know that it is physically impossible for this particular bond always to unite them. They must be aware that there is something more than that, something that must in the end transcend that physical union.

Looking at marriage from that point of view, can one desire that it should be anything less than permanent, indissoluble? That which God made, and, therefore, which no man should put asunder? Let the community—both Church and State—teach this. Let us make it clear that men and women should not marry unless they do sincerely believe that their love for each other is of this character. Let them understand that physical union should be the expression of a spiritual union. Let them learn that love, though it includes passion, is more than passion, and must transcend and outlive passion. And let us insist that all should learn the truth about themselves—about their own bodies and about their own natures—so that they may understand what they do, and may have all the help that knowledge can give in doing it. I hold that on such knowledge and such understanding the community should insist, if it is to uphold the high and difficult standard of indissoluble monogamous marriage. So only *can* it be rightly upheld.

I urge also that when a marriage takes place the State has a right and a duty with regard to it. For the sake of every citizen, and most of all for the sake of the children, it should "solemnize" marriage, and should do so on the understanding—clearly expressed—that those who come to be married intend to be faithful to each other "as long as they both shall live."

In doing this I believe the State does all—or nearly all—that it usefully can to uphold the dignity of marriage and a high standard of morality. I do not believe that it should seek to penalize those whose sex-relationships are not of this character, except so far as legislation for the protection of the immature or the helpless is concerned. And I do not think it should compel —or seek to compel, for compulsion is, in fact, impossible—the observance of a marriage which has lost or never had the elements of reality.

Is this to abandon the ideal I have been upholding? I do not think so. Let us refer again to the greatest of Teachers and the loftiest of Idealists—Jesus Christ. See what He teaches in the Sermon on the Mount and elsewhere. Everywhere He emphasizes the spiritual character of virtue and of sin. To be a murderer it is not necessary to kill: to hate is, in itself, enough. If you hate you are essentially a murderer. To be an adulterer it is not necessary to commit adultery: to look on a woman lustfully is already to have committed adultery with her in your heart. It is the spirit that sins. So keep your spirit pure. It is not enough to keep your oaths: you should be so utterly and transparently sincere that there is no need and no sense in supporting your words by great oaths. "Yea" and "Nay" should be sufficient.

You will notice that the Sermon on the Mount has been divided in this chapter into a number of paragraphs, each of which begins by a reference to the old external law of conduct, and goes on to demand a more searching, more spiritual and interior virtue. "Ye have heard that it was said by them of old time.... But I say unto you."

"Ye have heard that it was said: 'Thou shalt not kill' ... but I say unto you that whosoever is angry shall be in danger of the judgment. Ye have heard that it was said: 'Thou shalt not commit adultery,' but I say unto you that whosoever looketh on a woman to lust after her hath committed adultery with her already in his heart.... Ye have heard that it was said: 'Thou shalt not forswear thyself,' but I say unto you: 'Swear not at all.'"

What is the significance of such teaching? Surely that we are not to be satisfied with keeping the letter of the law, but are to keep it in our hearts. So clear is this that the Church has completely abandoned the letter of the last precept. No one except a Quaker refuses to take an oath. Every bishop on the bench has done so, and every incumbent of a living. Nowhere throughout the Sermon on the Mount have Christians felt themselves bound to a literal or legal interpretation of its teaching. No one wants a man to be tried for murder and hanged for hating his brother. No judge grants a divorce because a man or woman has "committed adultery in his heart." Christ Himself did not *literally* "turn the other cheek" when struck by a soldier. His disciples everywhere pray in places quite as public as the street-corners forbidden in the next chapter of St. Matthew, and give their alms publicly or in secret as seems to them best.

It may be contended that in this spiritual interpretation of Christ's commands it is very easy to go too far and "interpret" all the meaning out of them. It is certain, however, that the danger must be incurred, since nothing could make sense out of an absolutely *literal* interpretation. It would mean a *reductio ad absurdum*.

Apply such a literalism, for example, to the point at which for centuries the Church has sought to apply it—the indissolubility of marriage. It is admitted that since a phrase, of however doubtful authority, does make an exception in favour of divorce for adultery, the Church can recognize a law in this sense. But if we are to be literalists, it seems that a lustful wish is adultery! Is this to be a cause for divorce? And if not, why not? Obviously because we can no more apply such spiritual teaching literally than we can take a man out and hang him because he hates his brother! There we cease to be literal: how then can we fall back on a literal interpretation at another point?

I claim that there is no ground whatever for a more rigid and legal interpretation of our Lord's teaching about marriage than about taking oaths or praying in public. I believe that Christ held that marriage should be permanent and indissoluble, that only those people should marry who loved each other with a love so pure, so true, so fine as to be regarded rightly as a gift from God, who accepted their union as a great trust as well as a great joy, whose marriage might indeed be said to be "made in heaven" before it was solemnized on earth; but that He should insist on a legal contract from which all reality had departed, or regard as a marriage a union of which the most cynical could only say that it was made in hell, merely because the Church or the State had chosen to bless or register it, seems to me as unlike the whole of the rest of the Sermon on the Mount and as far from the spirit of Christ as east is from west. It surely is not conceivable that He to Whom marriage meant so much that He spoke of it as being made by God, Who conceived of the union of a man and woman as being the work of God Himself "Those whom God has joined together"—would have cared for the shell out of which the kernel had gone, for the mere legal bond out of which all the spirit had fled. Marriage should be indissoluble; but what is marriage? I heard a little while ago of a girl of 19 who was married to a man of 56. He was immoral in mind and diseased in body, and at the end of a year she left him with another man. He divorced her, and she is now married to that other man, and there are people who say that this marriage, which, so far as one can judge, is a moral, faithful, and a responsible union, blest with children who are growing up in a good home, is no marriage because the wife went through a ceremony with this other man before, and marriage is indissoluble. Marriage is indissoluble: "Those whom God has joined together let no man put asunder." Did God join those two together? They were married in a church. It is the Church that should repent in sackcloth and ashes for permitting such a mockery of marriage. Let the Church by all means do what it has so long failed to do, emphasize the sanctity of human relationships, make men and women realize how deep a responsibility they take in marriage, how sacred a thing is this creative love, from which future generations will spring, which brings into the world human bodies and immortal souls; which, even if it is childless, is still the very sacrament of human love. Let the Church teach all that it can to make marriage sacred and divine, but when it preaches that such a marriage as that is a marriage at all it does not uphold our moral standard but degrades it.

I have said enough before, I hope, to make you realize that I do not think that when passion has gone marriage is dead. I have seen marriages which seemed unequal, difficult, unblest, made into something lovely and sacred by the deep patience and loyalty of human nature, and believe it is the knowledge of such possibilities which makes Christian people, and even those who would not call themselves Christians, generally desire some religious ceremony when they are married. They know that for such love human nature itself is hardly great enough. They desire the grace of God to inspire their love for each other with something of that eternal quality which belongs to the love of God. I have seen husbands love their wives, and wives their husbands, with a divine compassion, an inexhaustible pity, which goes out to the most unworthy and degraded. Yes, I would even go so far as to say that unless you feel that you are able to face the possibility of change in the one you love, that you can love so well that even if they alter for the worse your love would no more disappear than the love of God for you would disappear when you change or fail, you have not attained to the perfect love which justifies marriage. But this is a hard saying, and, therefore, those of us who believe in God in any sense instinctively desire the blessing of God to rest on the undertaking of so great a responsibility. We want our love to be divine before we can undertake the whole happiness of another human being. Let the Church by all means teach this, and I believe that future generations will conceive more nobly and more responsibly of marriage for her teaching. But do not seek to hold together those between whom there is no real marriage at all. When seriously and persistently a man and a woman believe that their marriage never was or has now ceased to be real, surely their persistent and considered opinion ought to be enough for the State to act upon. Let no one be allowed to give up in haste. Let no one fling responsibility aside easily. Let it always be a question of long consideration, of advice from friends, perhaps even from judges. But I cannot help feeling that when through years this conviction that there is no reality in a marriage persists, this is the one really decent and sufficient reason for declaring that that marriage is dissolved. Let us have done with the infamous system now in force, by which a man and woman must commit adultery or perjury before they can get us to admit the patent fact that their marriage no longer exists as a reality. Let us have done with a system which makes a mockery of our divorce courts. I have the utmost sympathy with those who denounce the light way in which men and women perjure themselves to obtain release, but I affirm that the whole system is, in the main, so based on legalisms, so divorced from morality, that the resultant adulteries and perjuries are what every student of human nature must inevitably expect, however much he may regret and hate them. It will be in vain that laws are devised to prevent divorce by collusion, in vain that King's proctors or judges detect and penalize here and there the less wary and ingenious offenders. The law will continue to be evaded or defied. And the reason is fundamental: it is that the law is not based on reality. It affirms that a marriage still exists when it does *not* exist. It demands that two human beings should give to each other what they cannot give. And—the essence of marriage being consent—it makes the fact that both parties desire its dissolution the final reason for denying them! To force a woman to demand the "restitution of conjugal rights" when such "rights" have become a horrible wrong; to compel a man to commit, or perjure himself by pretending he has committed, adultery, before he can get the State to face the fact that his marriage is no longer a reality—is this to uphold morality? Is this the ideal of the Sermon on the Mount? Let us once for all abandon the pretence that *all* the marriages made in churches or in registrars' offices are, therefore, necessarily made in heaven. Let us get to work instead to see that the marriages of the future shall be made in heaven, and, above all, let us abolish the idea that a marriage is a real marriage which is based on ignorance, on fraud, on exploitation, on selfishness. Let us not dream that we can raise our standard of morals, by affirming that every mistake that men and women make in a matter in which mistaking is so tragically easy ought to imprison them in a lie for the rest of their lives. But let us take the ideal of Christ, in all its grandeur and all its reality, with our eyes fixed upon the ideal, but with that respect for human personality, that respect for reality and truth, which makes us refuse to accept the pretence that all the marriages we have known have been made by God. Let us, at least, in perpetuating such blasphemies as are some of the marriages on which we have seen the blessing of the Church invoked, cease to drag in the name of Christ to the defence of a system which has laid all its weight upon a legal contract, and kept a conspiracy of silence about the sacred union of body and soul by which God makes man and woman one.

VI

A PLEA FOR LIGHT

> Jesus said: "If any man walk in the day, he stumbleth not, because he seeth the light of this world. But if a man walk in the night, he

stumbleth, because there is no light in him."

My last address for the present[C] on the difficult questions that we have been considering here, Sunday after Sunday, is a plea for light.

[Footnote C: Another address was added a few weeks later in response to urgent requests.]

"Walking in darkness" has been, in sexual matters, the experience of most of us. Even now, in the twentieth century, it is not too much to say that most of us have had to fight our battle in almost complete darkness and something very near to complete isolation.

There are two great passions connected with the bodies of men and women, so fundamental that they have moulded the histories of nations and the development of the human race. They are the hunger for food and the instinct of sex. There is no other passion connected with our bodies so fundamental, so powerful, as these two; and yet, with regard to the second, most of us are expected to manage our lives and to grow up into maturity without any real knowledge at all, and with such advice as we get wrapped up in a jargon that we do not understand. We have been as those who set out to sea without a chart; as soldiers who fight a campaign without a map. I do not think this is too much to say of the way in which a large number of the men and women that I know—even those of this generation—have been expected to tackle one of the greatest problems that the human race has to solve.

May I sketch what I imagine is the experience of most people? At some point in our lives we begin to be curious; we ask a question; we are met with a jest or a lie, or with a rebuke, or with some evasion that conveys to us, quite successfully, that we ought not to have asked the question. The question generally has to do with the matter of birth—the birth of babies, or kittens, or chickens; some point of curiosity connected with the birth of young creatures is generally the first thing that awakens our interest. When we meet with evasion, lies, or reproof, we naturally conclude that there is something about the birth of life into the world that we ought not to know, and since it is apparently wrong of us even to wish to know it, it is presumably disgusting. We seek to learn from other and more grimy sources what our parents might have told us, and, learning, arrive at the conclusion that in the relations of men and women there is also something that is repulsive. And since, in spite of this, our interest does not cease but becomes furtive curiosity, we also conclude that there is something depraved and disgusting about ourselves.

Now, all of these three conclusions are lies; and, therefore, we set out in life equipped with a lie in our souls. It is not a good beginning. It means that almost at once those of us who persist in our desire to know are in danger of losing our self-respect. We learn that there is something in sex that is base—so base that even our own parents will not speak to us about it; and because of that, and because a child instinctively does accept, during the first few years of its existence, what its parents or guardians say, we assume that there must be something bad in us, since we so persistently desire to know what is so evil that nobody will speak of it at all. Or if anyone does allude to it, it is with unwholesome furtiveness and a rather silly kind of mirth, so as to increase in the minds of many of us the sense that there must be something in our nature that we cannot respect because nobody else finds it beautiful or respectable.

Our next step, especially if we are conscientious people, is to repress that something. And here I want to say a word in answer to a number of letters that I have had on the point which I raised early in this book, when I claimed that women have to pay as great a tax and suffer as great a hardship from repression as men do. People—both men and women—have written to say that this is not true, and to such I wish to make my point quite clear. I did not say that men and women suffered *in the same way*. I said that they suffered *equally*; and since the question has been raised, I should like just to answer it here. To me it seems, judging as far as I can, from the people that I know, that—speaking very generally—passion comes to a man with greater violence, and is more liable to leave him in peace at other times. Passion is to a man who is of strong temperament like a storm at sea. It seems the very embodiment of violence and force. The mere sight of the sea angry almost terrifies one, even if one is perfectly safe from the violence of the storm; but the depths are not stirred. And in the case of a woman I would take a different figure of speech altogether, and say that very often the strain on her is much less dramatic, much less violent, and more persistent. I think of the strain as something like that silent, uninterrupted thrust of an arch against the wall, of a dome on the walls that support it. There is no sign of stress. But it is so difficult to build a dome rightly that Italy, the land of domes, is covered with the ruins of those churches whose domes gradually, slowly, thrust outwards till the walls on which they rested gave way and the church was in ruins. That kind of strain is easily denied by the very people who are enduring it. It is so customary, so much a part of their life, that they are unconscious of it.

No one who studies psychology to-day can fail to realize how unconscious people often are of the seat and the nature of their own troubles. It is true that the tendency to *exaggerate* the importance of sex seems likely to vitiate to some extent the conclusions of psychologists like Freud and his disciples. But that they have revealed to us a mass of hitherto unknown and un-understood suffering in the minds of both women and men, arising from the continual repression of a passion whose strength may be measured by the disastrous consequences caused by repressing it, no one who knows anything at all of modern psychology can deny. Those who do not understand their own trouble will often deny that the trouble exists, and deny it quite honestly. But those who have become the physicians of the mind are just beginning to learn how tremendous a sacrifice the world has asked of women in the past while denying that it was a sacrifice at all!

Now, this repression follows, in many women and in a considerable number of men, on the assumption that there is something in sex too shameful to be spoken about or looked at in the light. We set out, I repeat, on our campaign without a map of the country and with our compasses pointing the wrong way. And this, above all, is true when repression has caused some actual perversion in the mind, some arrested development, some abnormal condition. This is not always the consequence of deliberate repression on the part of the individual, but it is, I believe, often the consequence of an artificial state of civilization; an attitude towards a great and wonderful impulse which has perverted our whole view of what is divine and lovely in human nature. Whatever the cause, the result is abnormality of some kind, and to people who have suffered so, I want, above all, to say this: light and understanding are needed more by you, perhaps, than by anyone else, and to you, above all, they have been denied. Loneliness, isolation, the loss of self-respect, the darkness of ignorance have surrounded those to whom the sacrifice has been hardest, and, therefore, the repression, whether racial or individual, most disastrous. You can, if you choose, leave the world a nobler place because you let light in on these dark places. Do not say to yourselves that your suffering is useless and purposeless because it is no good to anyone: no one knows of it: no one understands it: and, therefore, it has all the additional bitterness of being to no purpose. That need not be true. Ignorance need not continue. If you will try to make your suffering of service to the world, it is not difficult to measure how great may be our advance in fundamental morality in this present generation.

We do not know yet of what human nature is capable, and those who are studying the human mind are perhaps the greatest of all pioneers at the present moment. Some of you have trusted me, and by your trust have enabled me to help other people. Others of you, perhaps, have yourselves become or will become students of psychology. You will advance a little further in a science which is as yet only making its first uncertain steps. Even if you do none of these things, yet if you will try to understand yourselves, by the mere fact that you understand, you will find that you are able to help other people—other people whose condition is most tragic, most lonely—to face with courage the problem they share with you.[D] Try to solve it, as you can. You will gain in understanding and strength, so that those in yet greater need will instinctively come to you for help. Base your own moral standard on all that is noble, and wise and human, and you will find that in you the spiritual begins so to dominate the physical that others will see its power and come to you for help.

[Footnote D: This subject is more fully dealt with in the next chapter.]

"With aching hands and bleeding feet,
We toil and toil; lay stone on stone.
Not till the light of day return
All we have built shall we discern."

Now let us turn to the other side of the problem—the more normal relations of men and women who are lovers, who are husbands and wives. May I again recapitulate what appears to be the history of many married people, even in 1921.

Let me remind you first that this contract of marriage is the most important, probably, in the whole life of the man and woman who undertake it; that it concerns human personality as perhaps no other relation in the world does, so deeply, so closely, so intimately, that those who enter into it are very near either to heaven or hell. The nearer you come to any other human personality, the nearer you get to the supreme happiness or the supreme failure. And when people enter on this relationship, how are they prepared? Many of them are ignorant—and in the case of women often wholly so—of what marriage actually involves. I find it difficult to speak in measured terms of those parents who deliberately allow their daughters to take a step which involves the whole of their future life and happiness, and that of another human being also, in ignorance of what they are doing. This relationship, which requires all the love and all the wisdom of men and women—so much so that even those who do not call themselves Christians often desire to go to a church and ask for the grace of God to enable them to carry out so great an undertaking—is entered upon by people who literally do not know what, from the very nature of marriage, is required of them. I suppose many people will say that I speak of a state of things which passed a generation ago. No, I do not. I speak of a state of things that is only too common at this present time. I have known marriage after marriage wrecked by the almost unbelievable ignorance that has been present on both sides. I say both sides. First of all, there is the girl. To her, marriage comes sometimes as so great a shock that her whole temperament is warped and embittered by it. Then there is the man, equally ignorant—very often, probably less ignorant of himself, but equally ignorant of her—not realizing how she should be treated. They are often quite ignorant of each other's views on marriage; of what sort of claims they are going to make on each other; what each thinks about the duty of having children. These elementary facts of human life, which must confront those who marry, are faced by them without any kind of preparation, without the most rudimentary knowledge of each other's point of view. And that there are so many happy marriages in spite of all this makes one realize how extraordinarily loyal, fine and courageous, on the whole, human nature is.

Only the other day I was speaking in a town in the north of England on this very subject, and I got a letter afterwards to say that the writer had very greatly enjoyed my address at the time. She had found it, she assured me, inspiring and elevating. But she felt bound to write and tell me afterwards (what she was sure would both shock and distress me) that she had found that some of the people in my audience were actually acting on what I said! I suppose every public speaker comes up against that sort of thing sometimes—the calm assurance that you are merely talking in the air and have not the slightest desire that anyone should act on what you say. So this lady wrote to say that, though she and her husband had both been greatly impressed by what I said, they were horrified to find that, as a result, people were actually discussing with one another, before they married, certain points which she mentioned to me and which she said they ought never to discuss until they *were* married. Is it not amazing that anyone should seriously contend that it is better to arrive at an understanding with the person he or she is about to marry *after* marriage than before? That people who would not dream of betraying anyone into any kind of contract about which they were not satisfied that its terms were understood should be willing to betray others—I deliberately call it a betrayal—into a contract of such infinite importance, and positively desire that they shall be ignorant of its nature?

It really seems sometimes as if pains were positively taken to mislead those who are going to be married. One of the most amazing statements on this subject, for instance, is contained in the marriage service of the Church of England, where the bride and bridegroom are told that marriage was ordained that "such persons as have not the gift of continency might marry and keep themselves undefiled members of Christ's body." That there should be anyone in the twentieth century who does not know that a man or a woman who has not the gift of continency is totally unfit for marriage is really rather startling. What such a person requires is both a divine and a physician; but that he should be told that he is fit for marriage and that marriage was expressly designed for him is not only misleading, it is absolutely horrifying. It explains the tragic wreck which so many marriages become after a comparatively short time.

I would urge, then, for the future, that we should not concentrate all our moral, ethical, religious, and social force on perpetuating the tragic failure of an empty marriage, but, rather, should concentrate our efforts on trying to make people understand what marriage is; what their own natures are; what marriage is going to demand from them; what they need in order to make it noble. I urge, moreover, that the same principle should apply to those who do not marry—that they also should learn in the light what their difficulties are going to be; how to face their own temperaments; how to deal with their own minds and bodies. Your temperament, men and women, does not decide your destiny; it does decide your trials. To know how to deal with it and how to make it your servant, how so to enthrone spiritual power in your nature that it shall dominate all that is physical, not as something base, but as a sacred and a consecrated thing—it is on this that the teachers of to-day should concentrate with all their power. It is true that when we have learnt all that is possible from teaching, there is still something to learn. In marriage is it possible to know finally until the final step is taken? No, I do not think so. But when you consider how we have struggled against ignorance, how many pitfalls have been put in the path of those who desired knowledge, how we have, as it seems, done our best to make this relationship a failure, surely it is worth while, at least, to try what knowledge, and understanding, and education, and training *can* do. We cannot know all. That is no reason why we should not know all that we can.

Surely marriage must be a divine institution, since we have done so much to make it a failure, and yet one sees again and again such splendid love, such magnificent loyalty and faith! "You advocate," someone wrote to me the other day, "you advocate that people should leave each other when they are tired of each other." No, I do not advocate that anyone should accept a failure. I advocate that every human being should do all that is possible—more perhaps than is possible without the grace of God—to make marriage the noble and lovely thing it should be. I think those are faint-hearted who easily accept the fact that it is difficult, and from that drift swiftly to the conclusion that for them it is impossible. I advocate that the greatest faith and loyalty should be practised. I believe in my heart that there is perhaps no relationship which cannot be redeemed by the love and devotion and the grace of God in the hearts of those who seek to make it redeemable. What I do say is that in Church and State we should concentrate all our efforts on helping men and women to a wise, enlightened, noble conception of marriage before they enter upon it, and not on a futile and immoral attempt to hold them together by a mere legal contract when all that made it valid has fled.

I believe that the more one knows of human nature the more one reverences it. I believe that the vast majority of human beings strain every nerve rather than fail in so great a responsibility. Do you remember reading in Mr. Bertrand Russell's book, "Principles of Social Reconstruction," of a little church of which it was discovered, not, I think, very long ago, that, owing to some defect in its title, marriages which had been celebrated there were not legal? Mr. Bertrand Russell says that there were at that time I forget how many couples still living who had been married in that church, who found that, by this legal defect, they were not legally bound. Do you know how many of those married people seized the opportunity to desert each other and go and marry somebody else? Not a single one! Every one of those couples went quietly away to church and got married again!

Religious people do sometimes think such mean things of human nature, and human nature is, for the most part, so much nobler, so much more loyal, so much more loving than we imagine. "Lift up your eyes unto the hills from whence cometh your help." "He that walketh in the light, stumbleth not, for he seeth the light of the world."

Let us face the future courageously, with great reverence for other people's opinions and views. Let us not join that mob of shouters who are prepared to howl at everyone who desires to say something that is not quite orthodox, but which is their serious and considered contribution to a great and difficult problem. Let us greet them with respect, however much we may differ from them. Let us look forward without fear. Believe me, below all the froth and scum of which we make so much, human nature is very noble.

Let us give that example to the world which is worth a thousand arguments—the example of a noble married life, the example of a noble single life. Those of you who are alone can do infinitely more for virtue by being full of gentleness, wisdom, sanity, and love than by any harsh repression of yourselves. It is by what you can make of celibacy that the world will judge celibacy. And so of married lovers. Believe me, it is not the children of married lovers who are rebels against a lofty standard. Those who have seen with their eyes a lovely, faithful and unwavering love are not easily satisfied with anything that is less. "Lift up your eyes unto the hills. From whence cometh your strength." And in the light of a great ideal, in the light of knowledge, sincerity and truth, in the light of what I know of human nature, I, for one, am not afraid for the future moral standard of this country.

VII

FRIENDSHIP

"Saul and Jonathan were lovely and pleasant in their lives, and in their death they were not divided: they were swifter than eagles, they were stronger than lions. Ye daughters of Israel, weep over Saul, who clothed you in scarlet, with other delights, who put on ornaments of gold upon your apparel. How are the mighty fallen in the midst of the battle! Oh Jonathan, thou wast slain in thine high places. I am distressed for thee, my brother Jonathan: very pleasant hast thou been unto me: thy love to me was wonderful, passing the love of women. How are the mighty fallen, and the weapons of war perished!" (II. Sam. i. 23-27.)

"And Orpah kissed her mother-in-law; but Ruth clave unto her. And she said, Behold thy sister-in-law has gone back unto her people, and unto her gods: return thou after thy sister-in-law. And Ruth said, Intreat me not to leave thee, or to return from following after thee: for whither thou goest, I will go; and where thou lodgest, I will lodge: thy people shall be my people, and thy God my God: Where thou diest, will I die, and there will I be buried: the Lord do so to me, and more also, if ought but death part me and thee." (Ruth i. 14-17.)

People have sometimes discussed with me whether it is right to have as intense and absorbing a love for a friend of one's own sex as exists between lovers. The word "absorbing" is perhaps the difficulty in their minds. All love is essentially the same, and it has been pointed out that the great classic instances of great love have been almost as often between friends as between lovers. But the test of love's nobility remains the same. If it is in the strict sense "absorbing"—if, that is, it is exclusive, if it narrows one's interests instead of enlarging them, if it involves a failure in love or sympathy with other people, it is wrong—it is not in the true sense "love"; but if it enriches the understanding, widens interest, deepens sympathy—if, in a word, to love one teaches us to love others better, then it is good, it is love indeed. A friendship which is of such character that no one outside it is of any interest, a maternal love which not only concentrates on its own but wholly excludes all other children, even a marriage which ultimately narrows rather than widens and is exclusive in its interests, is a poor caricature of love. A young mother may, in the first rapture of her motherhood, seem wholly absorbed; but, as a matter of fact, she generally ends by caring more for *all* children because she loves one so deeply. Even lovers, after the first absorption of newly-discovered joy, must learn to share their happiness and the happiness of their home with others if it is not to grow hard and dull. And friends may easily estimate the worth of their friendship by the measure with which it has humanized their relations to all other human beings.

There is another test also for love: Does it express itself naturally and rightly? This test is much more difficult to apply. One may believe that all love is essentially the same, but it is certain that all human relationships are not the same, and, therefore, love cannot always be expressed in the same way; but it is not possible to lay down any exact rule between the sort of "expression" legitimate to each. Everyone must have suffered sometimes from a sense of having forced undesired demonstrations on other people, or having them forced on oneself. One's suffering in the first instance is intensified by the knowledge of the extremity of revolt created by the second. There is nothing, I suppose, more acutely painful than the sense of being compelled to accept demonstrations of affection to which one cannot in the same way respond. I believe that this shrinking from expressions which seem unnatural, is rightly intensified a hundredfold when the sense of wrongness or "unnaturalness" is due not to the individual but to the relationship itself.

The love which unites the soul to God, children to their parents, mothers and fathers to sons and daughters, lovers to one another, friend to friend, the disciple to his master, is all one. You cannot divide Love. But to each belongs its right and natural expression, and to parody the love of lovers between friends revolts the growing sense of humankind. The very horrors of prostitution create a less shuddering disgust than the debauching of a young boy by an older man, though with a tragically common injustice society is more apt to be disgusted by the unfortunate victim, bearing all the marks of his moral and physical perversion, than by the more responsible older man who profits by or even creates it.

Yet it is, as I have said, only by the *growing* sense of humanity that such things are condemned. They were not always so in every case. On the contrary it has sometimes been maintained that friendship between men was so much nobler than the love of men and women that even when it demanded physical expression it was still the finest of all human relationship. This idea was, of course, widely held by the Greeks during the noblest epochs of their history, and Plato, though he does not, as is commonly believed, justify such expression as good in itself, evidently regards it as practically inevitable and, therefore, to be condoned. And though from this indulgent attitude there has been a very general revolt in modern times, the reaction has not always been very discriminating in its condemnation or very just in its reprisals. Now—in consequence, no doubt, of this injustice—there has arisen another attempt to assert the superior nobility of friendship over love,[E] and even to claim a superior humanity for people who are more attracted by members of their own sex.

[Footnote E: I am using the terms "friendship" and "love" in their ordinarily accepted and narrow sense, as meaning respectively the love of friends and the love of lovers. This is arbitrary, but I cannot find other words except by using long phrases.]

There is not in this any question of the bestial depravity which deliberately debauches the young and innocent: it is a question of the kind of friendship glorified by Plato. And those who uphold the Platonic view are not always debauchees but sometimes men and women who, however incomprehensibly, still sincerely believe that they and not we who oppose them are the true idealists. This is why it is worth while to state our reasons for our profound disagreement, and to do so as intelligently and fairly as possible. It is also worth while because no one has suffered more cruelly or more hopelessly than those whose temperament or abnormality has been treated by most of us as though it were *in itself*, and without actual wrong-doing, a crime worthy of denunciation and scorn.

First, then, let it be remembered that the highest types humanity has evolved have been men and women who are really "human," that is to say who have not only those qualities which are generally regarded as characteristic of their sex, but have had some share of the other sex's qualities also. A man who is (if such a thing could be) wholly and exclusively male in all his qualities would be repulsive; so would a woman wholly and exclusively female. One has only to look at history to realize it. Compared with the exquisite tenderness and joy of a St. Francis of Assisi, the courage and determination of a St. Joan of Arc, the intellectual power of a St. Catherine of Siena or St. Theresa of Spain, the "brute male" who is wholly male, the "eternal feminine" with her suffocating sexuality seem on the one hand inhuman, on the other subhuman. It is not the absence of the masculine qualities in a man, or of the feminine qualities in a woman which raises them above the mass; it is the presence in power of both; and no man is truly human who has not something of the woman in him—no woman who has not something of the man. Here is a certain truth. And its supreme example is Christ Himself—Christ in Whom power and tenderness, strength and insight, courage and compassion were equally present—Christ Who is in truth the ideal of all humanity without distinction of race, class or sex.

This is true. But its truth has been misunderstood by teachers like Edward Carpenter. Beauty and strength in human nature as elsewhere depend on harmony, and in such characters as I have cited that harmony is found. For, in fact, there is no instance in nature of a male wholly male or a female entirely female. Even physically the elements are shared. And if we say with confidence that where these elements are most fully shared there is found the fullest humanity, we are not committed to adding that where the body has one predominating character and the spirit another there is something finer still!

For harmony of life and temperament the body should be the perfect instrument and expression of the spirit. When you have the temperament of one sex in the body of another, this cannot be. There is at once a disharmony, a dislocation, a disorder—in fact, a less perfect not a more perfect type. Humanity does, I believe, progress towards a fuller element of the woman in the man, the man in the woman, and the best we have produced so far confirm the truth of this. But it is not an advance to produce a type in which the temperament and the body are at odds. This is not progress but perversion.

It is the same consciousness of dislocation which makes us condemn homosexual practices. Here it is a dislocation between the means and the end. The instinct of sex, to whatever use it may have been put, is fundamentally the creative instinct. It is not by an accident, it is not as a side-issue, that it is through sexual attraction that children are born. And however sublimated, however enriched, restrained and conditioned, the creative power of physical passion remains at once its justification and its consecration. To use it in a relationship which must for ever be barren is "unnatural" and in the deepest sense immoral. It is not easy to define "immorality," because morality is one of the fundamentals which defy definition; but though it is not easy to define, it is not hard to recognize. All the world knows that it is immoral to prostitute the creative power of genius to mere commercialism, for money or for fame. No one can draw a hard and fast line. No one will quarrel with a great artist because he lives by his art, or because he will sometimes turn aside to amuse himself, his public, or his friends. Michaelangelo is not blamed because, one winter's afternoon, he made a snow-statue for Lorenzo de Medici! Yet all will admit that *merely* to amuse, *merely* to make money, *merely* to gain popularity is a prostitution of genius. Why? Because it is to put to another than its real purpose the creative power of a great artist.

In the same way, to use the power of another great creative impulse—that of sex—in a way which divorces it wholly from its end—creation on the physical as well as the spiritual plane—is immoral because it is "unnatural." Again and again it will be found to lead to a violent reaction of feeling—a repulsion which is as intense and violent as the devotion which was its prelude.

What then should those do who have this temperament? No one, perhaps, can wisely counsel them but themselves. They alone can find out the way by which the disharmony of their being can be transcended. That it can be so I am persuaded. That modern psychology has already made strides in the knowledge of this problem we all know. What is due to arrested development or to repression can be set right or liberated: what is temperamental transmuted. But I appeal to those who know this, but who have suffered and do still suffer under this difficulty, to make it their business to let in the light, to help others, to know themselves, to learn how to win harmony out of disharmony and to transcend their own limitations. Let them take hold of life there where it has hurt them most cruelly, and wrest from their own suffering the means by which others shall be saved from suffering and humanity brought a little further into the light. Who knows yet of what it is capable? Who knows what is our ultimate goal? It may be that out of a nature so complex and so difficult may come the noblest yet, when the spirit has subdued the warring temperament wholly to itself.

And to the others I would say this. If the homosexual is still the most misunderstood, maltreated, and suffering of our race, it is due to our ignorance and brutal contempt. How many have even tried to understand? How many have refrained from scorn? Other troubles have been mitigated, other griefs respected if not understood. But this we refuse even to discuss. We are content to condemn in ignorance, boasting that we are too good to understand. In consequence, though a few here and there have preached homosexuality as a kind of gospel, far more have suffered an agony of shame, a self-loathing which makes life a hell.

To be led to believe that one is naturally depraved!—to be condemned as the worst of sinners before one has committed even a single sin! Is that not the height and depth of cruelty? Do you wonder if here and there one of the stronger spirits among these condemned ones reacts in a fierce, unconscious egotism and proclaims himself the true type of humanity, the truly "civilized" man? How shall they see clearly whom we have clothed in darkness, or judge truly who are so terribly alone?

To have a temperament is not in itself a sin! To find in your nature a disharmony which you must transcend, a dislocation you have to restore to order, is not a sin! Whose nature is all harmony? Whose temperament guarantees him from temptation? Is there one here who is not conscious of some dislocation in his life that he must combat? Not one!

It is a disharmony to have an active spirit in a sickly body. It is a disharmony to have, like one of the very greatest of Christ's disciples, "a thorn in the flesh to buffet him." Who shall deliver us from this body of death? When you hear of a Beethoven deaf or of a Robert Louis Stevenson spitting blood, are you not conscious of disharmony? Where there is perfect harmony—*perfect*, I say—such a dislocation could not be. Epilepsy has been called "la maladie des grands," because some great ones have suffered from it. Perhaps St. Paul did. It is not possible to imagine Christ doing so. In Him there existed so perfect a harmony of being that one can no more associate Him with ill-health than with any other disorder or defect. Yet we do not speak (or think) with horrified contempt of the disharmony present in St. Paul or in Beethoven. Rather we reverence the glorious conquest of the spirit over the weakness and limitations of the flesh. Some of us have even rushed to the opposite extreme and preached ill-health as a kind of sanctity, in our just admiration for those who have battled against it and shown us the spirit dominant over the flesh.

But, it will be urged, ill-health is quite another kind of disharmony than vice. We are not responsible for it, and cannot be blamed.

I am not prepared to admit that this is altogether true, but I will not discuss it now. The point I want to make clear, if I make nothing else clear, is that to be born with a certain temperament is not in itself a sin nor does it compel you to be a sinner. "Your temperament decides your trials; it does not decide your destiny." It is no more "wicked" to have the temperament of a homosexual than to have the weakness of an invalid. It is difficult for the spirit to dominate and to bring into a healthy harmony a body predisposed to illness and disorder. The greater the glory to those who succeed! Let us confess with shame that in this other and far harder case we have not only ignored the difficulty and despised the struggler, but—God forgive us—have, so far as in us lay, made impossible the victory.

VIII

MISUNDERSTANDINGS

> "If there is one result or conclusion that we may pick out from the science of sex which has developed so rapidly of recent years, as thoroughly established and permanently accepted, it is that the old notion of the sinfulness of the sex process, *in se*, is superstitious, not religious; and must be discarded before ethical religion can assert its full sway over humanity's sex life. And, most assuredly, the conception narratives [of the New Testament], by retaining the sex process to the important extent of normal pregnancy and parturition, foreshadowed and hallowed this development of ethical thought. They make it clear that the Spirit of God and the spirit of woman, in conscious union, refuse to justify superstitious and paralyzing fears, refuse to allow that the sex process is irredeemable; they render possible and imperative the working out of the ethical problems directly concerned with sex."

Northcute: Christianity and Sex Problems, pp. 415, 416.

During the course of these addresses I have more than once, and with more than common urgency, pleaded for the light of knowledge, that we may in future not make so many disastrous mistakes from sheer ignorance and misunderstanding. I have been asked to say more definitely what "misunderstandings" I had in mind, and to discuss them with at least as much courage as I have so pressingly demanded from others.

The demand is just; and I feel the less able to disregard it because I have discussed these very difficulties with people whose lives have been wrecked by the ignorance in which they were brought up, or saved by knowledge wisely imparted before the difficulties arose. Knowledge cannot save us from hardship or difficulty; it cannot make us invulnerable to attack, or lift us above the ordinary temptations of ordinary mortals; but it can show us where we are going; it can guide us when we wish to be guided; it can save us, when we wish to be saved, from mistakes cruel to ourselves and often far more cruel to other people.

For instance: it is very generally believed that the struggle for continence is greatly eased by continual and even exhausting physical activity. To work hard—to work even to exhaustion—is believed by some to be a panacea. At our great public schools the craze for athleticism is justified on the ground that, even at the expense of the things of the mind, it does at least keep the boys from moral evil.

I believe this to be a mistake, and a mistake which is due to our looking at sex from a too purely physical point of view. It is, of course, imbecile to forget the physical, and deal with sex simply as a "sin"; but it is no less stupid to forget that our bodies and souls are intimately bound together, and that there is much more in passion than a merely physical instinct. As a matter of fact, a tired person is not immune from sex-hunger, and even an exhausted person is likely to find that, far from sexual feeling being exhausted too, it turns out to be the only sensation that will respond to stimulus at all. The exploitation of sexuality by our theatres and Press is not successful only in the case of the idle and the overfed; it finds its patrons also among those who are too tired to put their minds into anything really interesting from an intellectual or artistic point of view, but whose attention can be distracted and whose interest held by a more or less open appeal to the primitive instincts of sex. Tired people want to be amused and interested if possible; but they are not easily amused by anything that appeals to the mind, because they are tired. They want a sensation other than the customary one of fatigue, and the easiest sensation to excite is a sexual one. They get it thinly disguised, in a theatre or music-hall, more thickly disguised in the form of cheap fiction, or quite undisguised elsewhere. But the idea that sexuality is destroyed by fatigue is a very mischievous illusion which has misled and helped to destroy some of the most honest strivers after self-control. Such people will, with a touching belief in saws, seek to find in exhaustion relief from temptation. But it is not amusing always to feel tired. One desires at last something else—some other kind of feeling—and one is too tired to make an effort. But sexual sensation is easily excited, and in the end the unfortunate finds that he has yielded again. His hard fight has only ended in defeat, and he either abandons the advice as mistaken, or himself as hopelessly and uniquely depraved.

The truth is, of course, that what is needed is not physical exhaustion any more than physical idleness and overfeeding. What is wanted is hard and *interesting* work—work that absorbs one's mental as well as physical strength. A boy at a public school who really cares for games can pour his energies into them and appear a fine example of the system; a boy who, though games are compulsory, cannot interest himself in them at all, is not helped by being physically exhausted. If, then, he yields to a temptation the other has escaped, this need not be because he is more wicked or more weak. It may quite well be because the insistence on athleticism, which has been elevated into a cult, in our public schools, has supplied a real and absorbing interest for the one, but has merely used the physical capacity of the other without touching his mind or his spirit at all. When shall we learn that every human being is a unity, and that to ignore any part of it—body, mind or spirit—is idiotic? The muscular Christian who believes that continence is achieved by physical fatigue is as short-sighted as he who would treat the whole matter as a purely ethical problem. But the man or woman who works hard at some congenial and absorbing task—especially if it be creative work—finds the virtue of continence well within his grasp without exhaustion and without asceticism. It is because sex is essentially a creative—the creative—power in humanity that we have to direct its force into some more spiritual channel than mere physical labour, if we are to make ourselves its master.

Again, an increasing number of us believe that to master our physical impulses is possible; and that it has seemed impossible—at least, for men—in the past largely because so little knowledge and so little common-sense has been used in achieving mastery. Naturally, it was simpler to assume that it was impossible to control oneself than to find out how to make it possible, but as we grow more civilized we cease to be perfectly content with this simple plan, and begin to perceive its extraordinary injustices and brutalities. It has been said that the civilization of any people or period may be judged by the position of its women, and though this is too simple to be quite true, it is far more true than false. If, however, civilization does raise the position of women, and assign to them a greater freedom of action and a wider scope for their lives than was theirs before, it must be clearly understood that women in these circumstances and of this type will take a quite different line on the question of sex morals than their great-grandmothers did. It is, for example, still urged that women must not do this, that or the other work, because it involves working with men whose sex instincts may be uncontrollably aroused by such collaboration. Sir

Almroth Wright has pleaded this, and it is being urged to-day against the entrance of women into what is now almost the only sphere still closed to them—the spiritual work of the Churches. It is urged that some men are afraid of being sexually excited if they are addressed by a woman-preacher, and that others cannot be within the sanctuary, with a woman near them, without similar danger. The misunderstanding that arises here is, surely, that the cause of this abnormal excitement is in the woman, whereas (in the cases cited) it is in the man. There are, of course, women who find an exactly similar difficulty in working with men: women who are transformed by the mere presence of men, as there are men who cannot enter a room full of women without physical disturbance. Such men, such women, are not necessarily depraved or immoral persons, their temperament may be a source of genuine distress to them. It may be most admirably controlled, and in thousands of cases it is so, especially when the sufferer understands himself or—more rarely—understands herself. All the help that psychology and medical science can give (and it is much) should be given to and accepted by such people. The one thing that should *not* be yielded is the ridiculous claim that men and women who are not so susceptible (and who are in the vast majority) should rule their lives according to the standards of those who are sexually over-developed or one-sidedly developed. It cannot be too strongly insisted that this problem is the problem of the individual. He (or she) has got to settle it. He must learn to manage himself in such a way that he ceases to be abnormally excitable, or he must arrange his life so that he avoids, as far as possible, the causes of excitement. He must not expect others to cramp their lives to fit him; he must not expect civilization to be perverted or arrested in order to avoid a difficulty which is his own.

The only alternative to this is to revert to a form of civilization in which it was frankly admitted that sex-impulses could not be controlled, either by men or by women, and society was therefore organized on a basis which, quite logically, provided for the restraint of women in a bondage which prevented them from satisfying their impulses as they chose, and at the same time protected them from attack by other men than their lawful owners; and which, further, provided conveniences for the equally uncontrollable instincts of men.

This system is quite logical; so is the one here advocated, of assuming that the sexual instincts of both sexes can be controlled. What is not logical is the assumption that they *can* be controlled, but that such control is to be exercised not by each one mastering himself, but by the removal of all possibility of temptation! This demand is really incompatible with our civilization, and those who make it should try to understand that what they ask is, in fact, the reversal of all advance in real self-control in matters of sex.

Let us abandon the pretence that it is "wicked" for either a man or a woman to have strongly-developed sex-instincts. When we do this, we shall be on the high way to learning how to manage ourselves without making preposterous demands upon our neighbours or inroads upon their individual freedom.

We shall also, I believe, get rid of those perversions which darken understanding as well as joy. One need not go all the way with Freud—one may, indeed, suspect him of suffering from a severe "repression" himself—while admitting, nevertheless, that much of the folly that surrounds our treatment of sex-questions is due to the pathetic determination of highly respectable people to have no sex nature or impulses at all. Certainly this accounts for much that is called "prudery" in women, whose repressed and starved instincts revenge themselves in a morbid (mental) preoccupation with the details of vice. I am forced to the conclusion that it has also something to do with the quite extraordinary description that certain ecclesiastics give of their own inability to control their imaginations even at the most solemn moments. A narrow and dishonest moral standard has been foisted upon women in these matters, and instead of knowing themselves and learning to control their natures, they have been given a false idea of their own natures, and taught instead merely to repress them. So, very often, a curiously artificial code of manners has been accepted by the clergyman—a code which has been crystallized in a phrase by calling the clergy "the third sex"—and he, like the women, should be in revolt against it if he is to be saved. Indeed, we are or should be allies, not foes. Let the priest or minister wear the same kind of collar as other people, mix with them on equal terms, and then, if he has a higher moral standard than they, it will be his own standard, accepted by him because it commands his homage, and not a standard imposed on him merely because he belongs to a certain caste. It is always the code of morals imposed from without that does mischief, and results in the repressions and perversions about which modern psychology has taught us so much.

It will perhaps be urged that the peculiar dangers of which ecclesiastics are conscious are due to the psychological fact that the erotic and religious emotions are closely allied. That this is a fact will hardly be doubted. But again the problem is either an individual one, *or* it must be solved by abandoning our present position and reverting to that of an earlier and cruder civilization. It is possible to argue that eroticism and religion are so nearly allied and so easily mistaken for one another, that safety and sincerity alike demand separate worship for men and women.[F] It is also possible to leave it to the individual to manage himself, conquer where he can and flee where he cannot. But it is not possible, on grounds of religious eroticism, to protect men from listening to a woman preaching, at the cost of compelling women to listen to no one but a man; or insist on the intolerable cruelty of compelling a man-priest to celebrate mass with a woman server, while forcing the woman to make her confession to a man.

[Footnote F: As, *e.g.*, among the Mahometans and, to a less extent, the Jews.]

I am convinced that when religious people learn to refrain from cheap "religion" based on emotional preaching and sentimental or rowdy music, they will find that, though eroticism and religion are nearly allied and can easily be mistaken, it is not impossible to distinguish between them. The effort to do so should be made by our spiritual leaders, and when made will result in a sturdier and more thoughtful religion. While for those, whether men or women, who are honestly aware that for them certain things are impossible there will be an obvious alternative. The man who cannot forget the woman in the priest or preacher will not attend her church; the woman, of whom the same is sometimes true, will avoid the ministrations of men. There will then be less of that eroticism in religion which some of those who—by a curious perversion of logic—oppose the ministry of women actually quote as a reason for compelling women to go to men-priests because there is no one else for them to go to.

IX

FURTHER MISUNDERSTANDINGS: THE NEED FOR SEX CHIVALRY

> "Men venerated and even feared women—particularly in their specifically sexual aspect—even while they bullied them; and even in corrupt and superstitious times, when the ideal of womanhood was lost sight of, women tended to get back as witches the spiritual eminence they had failed to retain as saints, matrons and saviours of society."

Northcote: Christianity and Sex Problems, p. 326.

Chivalry is the courtesy of strength to weakness. Yet women who pride themselves on their superior moral strength in regard to sex rarely feel bound to show any chivalry towards the weak. I do not myself believe that women are *as a whole* stronger than men, or that men are *as a whole* stronger than women; but I am sure that the sexes are relatively stronger in certain respects and at certain points, and that where one is stronger than the other, that one should feel the chivalrous obligation of strength whether man or woman. Chivalry is not and ought not to be a masculine virtue solely.

For example, it is quite common to be told of (or by) some girl who is an artist in flirtation that she is "quite able to take care of herself." This appears to mean that whoever suffers, she will not; and whatever is given, she will not be the giver. It is possible to go further and say that whatever she buys she will certainly not pay for.

What does she buy? Well, it depends, of course, on what she wants and what is her social class. But, roughly speaking, she wants both pleasure and homage—not only theatres and cinemas, ice-creams or chocolates, but the incense that goes with such things—the demonstration of her triumphant sexual charm, which evokes such offerings.

Of course, in a great deal of this there is no harm. People who like each other will like to please each other, to give pleasure, and to enjoy it together. But there is something beyond this which is not harmless but detestable, and that is the deliberate playing on sexual attraction in order to extract homage and to demonstrate power. A girl will sometimes play on a man as a pianist on his instrument, put a strain on him that is intolerable, fray his nerves and destroy his self-control, while she herself, protected not by virtue but frigidity, complacently affirms that she "can take care of herself." The blatant dishonesty of the business never strikes her for a moment. She takes all she wants and gives nothing in return, and honestly believes that this is because she is "virtuous." That she is a thief—and one who combines theft with torture—never occurs to her; yet it is true.

Observe—I do not suggest that it would be creditable if she did "pay." It would be no more so than Herod's payment of John the Baptist's head. But although it is wrong to take something you want and give in return what you ought not to give, it would be a curious sort of morality that would go on to argue that it is right to take all and give nothing. Both transactions are immoral and one is dishonest.

On the other hand, it must be remembered that a parasite *must* take all and give nothing or as little as possible. That is the law of its being. And so long as men resent the independence of women, and enjoy the position of perpetual paymaster, so long will many women be driven to use the only weapon they have left. Moreover, it is fair to say—and this is why I plead for light—that many of them are genuinely ignorant that they are playing with fire. The more frigid they are themselves, the less are they able to gauge the forces they are arousing; the more ignorant they are, the less possible is it for them to be chivalrous to those whose strength and weakness they alike misunderstand. The half-knowledge, the instinctive arts, which girls sometimes display continually mislead men into thinking them a great deal cleverer than they are. Each is ignorant of the other's weakness, and each puts the other in danger because of that ignorance.

I once spoke to a big meeting of girls in the neighbourhood of a big camp, during the war; and reflecting on the difficult position of the men—their segregation from ordinary feminine society, their distance from their homes, their unoccupied hours, and the inevitable nervous and emotional strain of preparing for the front—I tried to make the girls realize how hard they could make it for the men to keep straight, if they were ignorant or foolish themselves. I knew—and said so—that the girls were in a difficult position too; but, after all, they prided themselves on being the more "moral" (*i.e.* the stronger) sex, and should be chivalrous.

Afterwards I got a reproachful letter from a woman-patrol, who assured me that if anything went wrong, it was not the fault of the girls. "They are a rough lot," she wrote, "and, of course, they like to have a soldier to walk out with. They like to romp with the men, and to kiss them, and perhaps they do go rather far in letting the men pull them about. But they have no intention whatever of going any further. If things do go further, it is the men's fault, not the girls'."

I could hardly have a better instance of the sort of thing I mean. The girls want to have "fun" up to a certain point, and there stop. It does not occur to them that there may be a difference in the point at which they propose—or wish—to stop, and that at which the man can. That there is any physiological or psychological factor in the case which makes stopping possible at one moment and next-door to impossible at another, and that these factors may differ between the sexes, so that one cannot stop just where the other can, is quite a new idea not only to factory girls but to women-patrols—at least to some of them. A girl will cheerfully start a man rushing down an inclined plane and then complain because he continues rushing till he reaches the bottom. Well, in a sense, we ought not to complain of either of them: we ought to challenge the senseless way in which they are kept in the dark about each other.

In these days, when so much greater liberty is accorded to boys and girls than was given in the past, the friends of liberty should insist with obstinacy on the need for knowledge. For if liberty is unaccompanied and unguided by knowledge, its degeneration into licence will be triumphantly used by the lovers of bondage as an argument against liberty itself. Let me then say boldly that I am all for liberty. I want boys and girls, men and women, to see far more of each other and get to know each other much better than in the past. I believe in co-education, and in *real* co-education—not the sham that is practised in some of our universities and colleges. I see the risks and I want to take them. I know there will be "disasters," and I think them much less disastrous than those attending the methods of obscurantism and restraint. I think the idea that a boy and girl may not touch each other introduces a silly atmosphere of unreal "romance" where commonplace friendship is what is wanted. But with all this, and *because* of all this, I want a girl to know that a boy's body and mind are not *exactly* like hers; and perhaps a boy to know that a girl's is not totally *unlike* his!

In what way do they differ? The male, I think, is more liable to sudden gusts of passion, of violence so great as to be almost uncontrollable—at least so nearly so as to make it both cruel and stupid to arouse them. A woman's nature is not (generally) so quickly stirred. She takes longer to move (hence the universal fact of courtship). Or rather it might be more accurate to say that he and she may both start at the same time from the same point, but she takes longer to reach the end, and because this is so, is more capable of stopping before the end is reached. This she does not understand, and expects that if *she* can pause, so can *he*; while he also misunderstands, and does not know that there is for her, just as much as for him, a moment when self-control becomes impossible.

I have said so much about the lack of chivalry shown by women to men that it is only reasonable to point out that the reverse is true, and that men are often extraordinarily unchivalrous towards women. The cause is, of course, the same: they do not realize what a strain they are putting on them. There is still a very general assumption, even by those who really know better, that women have no passions and are untempted from within. I have often been assured by "men of the world" that "a woman can always stop a man if she wants to." No doubt she can—some men. She can "stop them if she wants to." The trouble is that a time comes when she cannot want to. The bland assumption that a man has a perfect right to play on a woman's sex-instincts till they are beyond control, and then call her the guilty one because they *are* beyond control, is based on the age-old determination not to recognize the full humanity of women. They are "different" from men. So they are. I have admitted it. But the likeness is much greater than the difference. And neither the likeness nor the difference makes self-control an easy thing for her. It is easier up to a certain point, because she is more slowly moved; it is harder when that point is reached because her whole nature is involved. She has never learnt to say that she can give her body to one while remaining spiritually faithful to another, and perhaps she never will learn. I at least suspect so. She may be as fickle as a man, but it will be in a different way.

Of course, in all this I generalize very rashly from a very narrow experience. My excuse is that these things must be discussed if we are ever to generalize more safely, or to learn that we must not generalize at all. And I have come to the conclusion that it is perhaps as possible to know something of what is or is not true when one is unmarried as when one is married. At least one escapes the snare into which so many married people surprisingly fall, of generalizing from an experience which is not merely as narrow as everyone's must be, but actually unique; which enables them to pronounce with stupefying confidence that all men are as this man is; all women as his wife; and all marriages as his marriage. When one has had the honour of receiving the confidence of a succession of such prophets and heard them pronounce in turn, but in an entirely different sense, upon the difficulties or easinesses of sex-relationships, always with a full assurance that they are right, not only in their own case but universally, one begins to make a few tentative generalizations oneself in the hope that they will at least provoke discussion and engender light.

X

"THE SIN OF THE BRIDEGROOM"

> "A deathless bubble from the fresh lips blown
> Of Cherubim at play about God's throne
> Seemed her virginity. She dreamed alone
> Dreams round and sparkling as some sea-washed stone.
> Then an oaf saw and lusted at the sight.
> They smashed the thing upon their wedding night."
>
>   *Dunch,*
> *Susan Miles.*

Something has been said by others of one of the most fruitful sources of misunderstanding between men and women, where misunderstanding is likely to have the most disastrous results—what has been called by Rosegger "the sin of the bridegroom." Perhaps "sin" is a mistaken word. If irreparable harm is often done on the wedding night, it is quite as much due to ignorance as to cruelty. Nothing is more astonishing than the widespread ignorance of men *and women* of the fact that courtship is not a mere convention, or a means of flattering the vanity of women, but a physiological necessity if there is to be any difference at all between the union of lovers and a rape.

It is all, I suppose, part of the old possessive idea which, making of a woman something less than a human personality with wishes, desires and temperament of her own, forbade the man to realize or even to know that her body has its needs as well as his, and that to regard it merely as an instrument is to be in danger of real cruelty.

You can bargain for the possession of a violin and the moment it is yours, may play upon it. It is yours. If you are in the mood to play, it must be ready for you. If it is not, then tune it, and it will be.[G] But a human being cannot be treated so in any human relationship. It needs mutual patience and mutual respect to make a relationship human.

[Footnote G: But even a violin will need to be tuned.]

This simple fact, however, has been so little understood of lovers, that husbands have, in genuine ignorance of the cruelty they were committing, raped their wives on their wedding night. Judging by what one knows of wedding-days, it could hardly be supposed that there could be a more unpropitious moment for the consummation of marriage. And when to the fatigue and strain of the day is added—*as is still quite often the case*—blank though uneasy ignorance as to what marriage involves, or the thunderbolt of knowledge (*sic*) launched by the bride's mother the night before, or the morning of the day itself, it would be difficult with the utmost deliberation and skill better to ensure absolute repulsion and horror on the part of the bride. I think that any man who would consider this from the bride's point of view would see that she need not necessarily be cold or unresponsive because, in such circumstances, she needs rest and consideration more than passion. But I wish men could know a little more than this, and understand that to enforce physical union when a woman's psychical and emotional nature does not desire it, is definitely and physically cruel. Woman is not a passive instrument, and to treat her as such is to injure her.

Perhaps I may be forgiven for labouring this point because, in fact, misunderstanding here is so disastrous. Marriage, after all, is a relation into which the question of physical union enters, and if there is no equality of desire, marriage will be much less than it might be. Women are—idiotically—taught to believe that passion is a characteristic of the depraved woman and of the normal man, who is shown by this fact to be on a lower spiritual level than (normal) woman. This senseless pride in what is merely a defect of temperament where it exists has poisoned the marital relations of many men and women, and has led women into marrying when they were temperamentally unfitted for such a relation, and quite unable to make anyone happy in it. Nor ought they to be too much blamed, since they are often unaware of what they ought to be prepared to give in marriage and firmly convinced that their preposterous ignorance is in some inexplicable way a virtue. Why it should be admirable, or even commonly honest, to undertake duties of whose nature you are ignorant, neither men nor women seem ever to have decided, and the illusion is beginning to pass. But it is still not understood that the woman who is not temperamentally asexual may easily be made so by being forced when she is not ready, and physically hurt when a little patience and tenderness would have saved her. Forel, Havelock, Ellis and others have insisted on this, but their books are unfortunately not easily accessible to the general public; and something may be added to the more widely read productions of Dr. Stopes.[H] Not only the physiological but the psychological side of the problem has to be considered, and it would be hard to decide which is the more important or which the *vera causa* of the other's reaction. Scientists may perhaps tell us some day: here I want only to point out that there is a spiritual factor in the case which needs at least to be recognized.

[Footnote H: *Married Love*, *Wise Parenthood*, and *Radiant Motherhood*. By Marie Carmichael Stopes.]

Is passion a cause or an effect? In other words, should physical union be the expression of spiritual union? Is it the "outward and visible sign of an inward and spiritual grace?" Or is it a means by which that grace is achieved? I think the first instinct of most women would be to say that spiritual union should be *expressed* by physical union, and that unless this spiritual union exists the physical union is "wrong." And yet everyone who stops to think will admit that the expression of an emotion deepens it. One can "work oneself up into a rage" by shouting and swearing. One can deepen love by expressing love. It is noticeable that the whole case for birth control has repeatedly been argued from the ground that the act of physical union not only expresses but intensifies and increases love.

Marriage is the most difficult of human relations, because it is the most intimate and the most permanent. To live so close to another—who, in spite of all, *remains* another—to be brought so near, to associate so intimately with another personality, without jarring or wounding—that is hard. No wonder it is not invariably a success! But passion makes it possible to many to whom, without this, it would not be possible. Ultimately passion should be transcended since in any case it must be left behind. Yet it has served its end, in deepening and intensifying the love of two people for one another.

Where then lies the difficulty, since probably men and women alike would agree that what I have said is true?

The difference of view is perhaps more in practice than in theory; yet it is all the harder of adjustment for that. In theory, both men and women would agree that physical union, ideally, should express a spiritual union; and that in doing so, it deepens and intensifies it. But it is still possible to disagree as to which of these two aspects of an admitted truth is the more vital and fundamental.

It may be, as I have already suggested, that the woman's point of view is due to her physiology; or it may at least be influenced by it. At least, I am convinced that to the woman the sense that physical union is *only* justified by already existent spiritual union, is the normal one. I believe that, however incapable she may be of explaining it, and however her power of reasoning may be vitiated by wrong ideas about the sexual relation, she does instinctively recoil from its use when its reason for existence is not there. She may attribute her reluctance to the fact that she is too womanly (*sic*), too spiritually minded to have any desire for sexual relations at all; her husband may attribute it to coldness of temperament or "modesty." In fact, it is due to the cause I have stated, and if she had never been called upon to give her body except when her own desire for the "outward and visible sign" of an "inward and spiritual grace" demanded it, her husband would have found that she was not temperamentally defective, but as good a lover as he.

No one who lives in the world at all can fail to understand that in every human relationship, and supremely in this one, there must be much mutual accommodation, much give and take, a great gentleness to every claim made in the name of love. All I am concerned to do here is to help to clear up misunderstandings. It is no claim that I put forward that the woman's point of view is superior to the man's: merely that they seem to me a little different.

A man who is conscious of jarring, who finds himself a little at cross-purposes with the woman he loves, and yet knows that the jarring is merely superficial and the love profound, may easily feel that to ask and offer once more the supreme expression of that love is the best way to transcend the temporary lack of sympathy and restore love to its right place and true proportion. Who shall say that he is wrong? Is it not certain that the expression of love does intensify and deepen love? Is not a sacrament the means of grace as well as its symbol.

Yet let him be warned. He may easily seem to his wife to be contenting himself with the symbol without the reality, the body without the soul. If she understands him, she may go with him. If she does not, no yielding on her part—no physical passion that he may arouse—will quite stifle the protest which tells her that she suffers spiritual violation. Do you remember the cry of Julie in "The Three Daughters of M. Dupont"? "*It is a nightly warfare in which I am always defeated.*" That her physical nature is suborned to aid in the conquest only increases for her the sense of degradation.

This difference in point of view affects the relations of men and women far more widely than is realized, since it is apt to arise wherever the physical comes in at all—and where does it not? Not a touch only, or a caress, but all deliberate appeal to sexual feeling becomes more difficult to women as they grow more civilized. It is perhaps difficult for a man to realize, in the atmosphere of giggles and whispers with which sex is surrounded in the theatre, the novel and the press, how revolting it becomes to modern women to be expected to use such means for "holding" a lover, or extorting concessions from one who is "held." It was much easier, I suppose, when women did not understand what they were about. One sees that to such women it is comparatively easy to-day. And the position is complicated by inheritance of the age-old conviction that a woman is supremely woman when she can bend a man by precisely these means. But the revolt is here. And—for the sake of clearness—what I am concerned to show is that a woman is not necessarily asexual or cold because she will not use an appeal to sexuality in order to get what she wants. She may have all the "temperament" in the world, but she has also self-respect, and she revolts from the idea of exploiting for advantage what should be sacramental.

I believe that a better understanding on this point would save not only great disasters but an infinity of small jars and strains, and if I have put the woman's point of view at some length it is partly because I understand it better, but chiefly because it is comparatively "modern" to admit that she has a point of view to put.

Once understood, it becomes easier to understand also the startling successes and disastrous failures which attend the remarkable practice of "teaching a woman to love after she is married." The extent to which social tabus and prudery may actually inhibit a woman's natural sexual development makes it possible, as we have seen, for her to marry in ignorance of what marriage implies. When this happens, her love, though it may be noble, altruistic and spiritual, does not involve her whole nature. Her husband, if he respects her sufficiently, will be able to awaken that which sleeps, and in accordance with the undoubted truth that expression intensifies love, he does "teach her to love" him not only in one sense but in all.

On the other hand, if she does not already love him, he will not succeed in "teaching" her anything but disgust if he dreams that by compelling physical union he can create spiritual union.

Evidently it is a singularly dangerous attempt! It is to be hoped that in future no woman will run such risks out of ignorance, but that lovers will, before they marry, understand what each expects, what each desires to give, and at least *start* fair.

This is no less important with regard to other matters in which marriages are often wrecked. Surely people who propose to spend their lives together ought to know (for example) whether children are desired and whether many or few; and what the attitude of either is on the vexed subject of birth control. Imagine the case of a husband who thinks the use of contraceptives right and wishes to use them; and a wife who thinks them absolutely wrong and, being warned by the doctor that she must not have more children, cheerfully, and with perfect conviction that she is acting nobly, invites her husband to run the risk of causing her death! Yet I have known such cases.

I do not enter into the question of birth control, because it has been and is being discussed much more freely than in the past, and by married people who are much better able to estimate the difficulties and advantages on either side of the question than any unmarried person can possibly be. Since, however, I am continually asked at least to give my personal opinion, for what it is worth, and since it is true that I have heard a good deal (on both sides) from those who *are* married, I will say briefly that it seems to me of supreme importance (1) that every child that is born should be *desired*, and (2) that no mother's time and strength should be so far overtaxed as to prevent her giving to each child all the love and individual care that it requires.

This necessitates control of the birth-rate, for a baby every year means a too-hurried emptying of the mother's arms. But I disagree—very diffidently—with the majority of my friends and acquaintances who hold that the right and best method is the use of contraceptives. I do not think it the best; I do not think it ideal. Unlike some authorities who must be heard with respect, I can say with confidence that some of the noblest, happiest and most romantic marriages I know base their control of conception not on contraceptives but on abstinence. They are not prigs, they are not asexual, they do not drift apart, and they have no harsh criticism to make on those who have decided otherwise. These are facts, and it is useless to ignore them.

On the other hand, it is equally true that sometimes such an attempt at self-control leads to nervous strain, irritability and alienation. These also are facts.

Personally, I would submit marital relations to the two tests I have proposed, and add that we have succeeded in oversexing ourselves to an extent which cannot be ignored; that we have "repressed" till we are obsessed; and that, before we right ourselves, we shall have to make many experiments, try many roads, and suffer many things. It is then above all necessary that we be very gentle to one another and even a little patient with ourselves. I conceive it much better to use contraceptives than to bear unwanted children; I conceive it also better to use them than to be cruel to others or become neurotic oneself; but that it is the ideal I do not believe.

XI

COMMON-SENSE AND DIVORCE LAW REFORM

"Those whom *God* hath joined together let no man put asunder."

In view of what I have said[I] about our marriage and divorce laws, several people have asked what I should actually propose in the way of reform, and I am glad to take the opportunity of a new edition briefly to answer this question.

[Footnote I: See Chapter V.]

I do not wish to see reform take the line of a longer list of "causes" for divorce, such, for example, as drunkenness, insanity, imprisonment for life, and so on. I should prefer to abolish these lists altogether, and to bring all divorce cases under some form of "equitable jurisdiction," each case being decided on its merits.

It should be the business of the court to decide whether the marriage desired to be invalidated has *in actual fact* any validity or reality at all; and to declare the couple divorced if it has not. In such courts men and women (or a man and a woman) should act together as judges.

It will be urged that to decide such a question is beyond the power of any human judgment; but I submit that in fact such decisions are being given every day. A judge who grants a judicial separation is deciding that *a marriage has ceased to be real or valid*, and he divorces the couple *a mensa et thoro*, though leaving them without the power to marry again. He actually "puts them asunder" more rigidly than a divorced couple. Since this is possible, it cannot be impossible for him to decide that the marriage must be wholly dissolved, with freedom of re-marriage to other partners; though such a decision, being even more grave, should not be reached without certain safeguards.

These safeguards should include that teaching about marriage on which I have insisted throughout the whole of this book. Young people should know what sex is and involves: what marriage is: how necessary to the welfare of the race, their children and themselves are fidelity and love. They should know that unless they believe that their love is indeed for life they ought not to marry. They should understand that to fail here is to fail most tragically.

If, nevertheless, a man and woman believe that their marriage is a complete and hopeless failure, their claim to be released from it should not be granted in haste. A period of years should in any case elapse before divorce can be obtained, and every effort should be used to reconcile the two, to remove any removable cause of difficulty, to convince them of the possibility of making good, by loyalty, unselfishness and a deep sense of responsibility, even an incomplete and desecrated bond.

If, however, it is clear that for no worthy consideration can they be induced to take up again the duties and responsibilities of marriage—if they remain immovably and rationally convinced that their marriage is not a real marriage—they should be released. And this because it is not moral but immoral, not Christian, but unChristian, to pretend that a marriage is real and sacred *when it is not*.

If there is one quality more striking than another in the teaching of Christ, it is His emphasis on reality. It is in this that the height and depth of His morality stand revealed. We do no service—we do a profound disservice—to morals when we admit that a marriage is so utterly devoid of reality that the best thing we can do for a "married couple" is to separate them from each other altogether—set them apart—free them from each other's "rights"—break up their home—and yet maintain the legal lie that they are still a married couple.

It will be asked how the interests of the children can be safeguarded. The interests of children are best safeguarded by the education and enlightenment of parents. They cannot be wholly saved if, after all, their parents have ceased to love or respect one another, for nothing the law can do will make up to them for that which is every child's right—a home ruled by love and full of happiness. The best that can then be done is to rescue them from the misery of a home full of unhappiness and hatred, and to assign them to the parent who, in the judgment of the court, is best fitted to care for them.

Let me add that, while I hold that the persistent and unconquerable conviction of two people that they ought to be divorced ought ultimately to entitle them to it, this should not be the case if one only of two married people seeks release. In this case, the decision should be entirely with the court.

To those who feel that not only our Lord's words but also the interpretation put upon those words by the Church is of supreme importance, the following statement will be of interest: "It is quite arguable that relief may be granted on the grounds that what is impossible cannot be done. It may be shown on the one hand that to such and such a person it is morally impossible to live with such and such another person, and on the other hand that it is morally impossible to live without marriage. In such instances there is room for the exercise of our 'dispensation from the impediment of the legamen' (bond). This is the practice of the Eastern Church, which allows the innocent party to re-marry, and also grants relief in cases of incurable insanity."

With regard to the Western Church, "Divorce and subsequent re-marriage in pre-Reformation days were only allowed on grounds existing before the contract was entered into. (There seems good reason for the belief that our Lord's words as recorded by St. Matthew refer to prenuptial unchastity.) But in spite of this apparently narrow restriction there were fourteen grounds on which a marriage could be declared null and void before the Reformation, and it was constantly being done. Canonists and Theologians taught that the full and *free* consent of parties was essential to marriage—which teaching obviously would enable a very wide view of the subject to be taken."[J]

[Footnote J: From a "Memorandum on Divorce," published in *The Challenge,*
July 5, 1918.]